Tide being a fool

O.L. HALL

Tide being a fool

IVC Books

Published by:
IVC Books
Norfolk, Virginia 23501

This is a work of fiction. It is not meant to depict, portray, or represent any particular gender, real persons, or a group of people. All the characters, incidents, and dialogues are products of the author's imagination and are not to be construed as real. Any resemblance to actual events or persons, living or dead, is purely coincidental.

Library of Congress Control Number: 2007904762

ISBN: 9780615699899

Reprint 2015

Front cover design by Pamela Thomas

This book is dedicated to my mother, the late Ida Cade.

Ma, I know that you are looking down at me
and getting a good laugh.
I miss your laughter.
Rest in peace.
Love always.

Acknowledgments

I would like to thank my Heavenly Father for all his many blessings.

A special thanks to Zorena Nlewen, you were my number one supporter; Gail Martin, you stayed with me since day one; a special friend, Jean Wyche; my best friend, Debbie Hardy; and my sister in Christ, Schnetta Braxton.

I am grateful to Terry Smith, an avid reader, and Yolanda Taylor and Roderick Briggs for being there for me and giving me their honest opinions after reading the first few chapters.

I gratefully acknowledge my co-workers: Marquita Bennett, Charles and Bridgett Bristol, Alton Christmas, Emma Cornelius, Dexter Foriest, Kim James, Christine Nelson, Danielle Sargent, Laneka Waters, Sheila Wilkins, and Lisheena Williams,

I am thankful for the following persons who encouraged me to keep writing: Wanda Bazemore, Carla Burton, Freda Sumner, Sharon Franklin, Jonhtan Justice, Kim Kellebrew, Danesha Factor, the Epps family, Joyce Williams, William and Shirle Smith, April Williams, Beverly Lake, Margaret Walker, Dorothy Archie, Kathy Lea, Wanda Boyd, Clarence and Joyce Samples, Lisa Wright, Alvin and Deborah Wright, Yolanda Butts, Bennie Darvine and family, and Yolaine Williams—owner of VIP Beauty Salon in Portsmouth, Virginia.

I extend my profound gratitude to everyone who helped me. If I omitted any of your names, believe me, it was not intentional. Your name may not be listed, but I will always remember your generosity.

I could not have made it through this project without the love and support of my family especially my Goddaughter Felita Steverson...you are always there for me; my siblings Shirlene, Valarie, Zachary, Robin, Diane, Sheila, Carla, Tonia, and Dana; my brother-in-law Clifton; my nephew Michael Smith—remember...education is the key, hang in there, stay in school; and my future son-in-law, Errick Gaines.

Finally special praise to: my daughter Arkia who helped me with my typing...Ma loves you so much; my father Frank Cade; and the love of my life—my husband Ed, for believing in me. I thank you for your encouragement, your patience, and your love!

Contents

Meet the Girls

I am **Dasha Johnson**, hairstylist and owner of *Looking Good Beauty Salon*. Whatever Mike wants—Mike gets. I love him and cherish the ground he walks on. I almost put my business and finances in jeopardy to be with him.

My name is **Patricia (Pinkeye) Miller**. I still live in the projects—trying to make ends meet. My friends describe me as a fast talker and a hustler—and it's no joke when it comes to making money. I keep an old player on the side, but I am really in love with Duce, who is married and lives three units down from me.

I am **Jayela (Jaye) Scott**, a college graduate with a degree in social work. I don't give a damn about a man—if his money ain't right, then I ain't right—until lust, lies, and betrayal open my eyes.

My name is **Monetta (Monay) Taylor**. I am single and ready to live my life. I have a nursing degree and work as an operating room nurse. Maleake is the love of my life. I will do anything to be with him until—his betrayal and lies.

We have been friends since the seventh grade—and we vow to stay friends until death do us part. Our lives together in Norfolk, Virginia have been very interesting. Let us tell you about it.

Tide being a fool

Sisters in Crisis

"What's up Monay? Girl, I'm tired of leaving messages for you and you're not returning my calls. Oh, I know that Maleake's got your head sprung. Hit me back when you get this message."

Monay stepped out of the shower feeling down as usual after being lied to—again—by Maleake. Last night, he didn't show-up for their date to a concert. He had even purchased the concert tickets three months in advance. Monay looked at her caller ID. "Oh no! Jaye called. I would hate for her to find out that Maleake did not take me to the concert."

Her phone rang. It was Jaye calling back. Monay hesitated answering, but Jaye wasted no time telling her about Maleake.

"Hello Monay, this is Jaye. Girl, let me hit you in the head with this. I saw Maleake, at the concert last night, with a red-bone who thought she was the bomb! Maleake tried to act like he didn't see me, but of course you know I made myself known. I walked up like I was going to buy a drink and said, "Well hello Maleake. I see you're up to your old no-good tricks, again."

He grabbed that bitch's arm and said, "There you go Jaye, always in somebody's business."

I stood in front of that red-bone, looked her straight in the eye and said, "I know that's right".

"Girl you need to get rid of Maleake..."

Monay interrupted. "Jaye, let me hit you back. I got another call."

It was Pinkeye. "Hey Monay, girl. Duce's stupid wife keeps calling my house hanging up. She must be out of her mind playing games with me. I told her that maybe if she cleaned up her nasty house, her man might stay home. Do you know she had the nerve to call the rent office on me—talking about I run a gambling house. I told that bitch that when I see her, I'm going to kick her in her ass."

~

Jaye stopped by Pinkeye's house. Through the screen door, she saw Pinkeye looking spaced out, sitting at the kitchen table. "What's up Pinkeye?"

"Girl, Harold just left my house talking stuff to me. He told me that he didn't have no money for me because he had to pay for his car to be fixed. But Shay, who lives down the street, told me that Harold ain't got no money cause he be trickin' with Pea—you know the project whore. You know I don't play that old player talk, but this time I let Harold walk out of my house without giving me a dime. Am I loosing my touch?"

"Naw girl," Jaye answered. "You know you still..."

Duce walked in and Jaye stopped talking.

"Hi lady."

"Hi Duce," said Jaye as she rolled her eyes at him.

Now that's what Pinkeye needs to get rid of. How can she be such a fool over someone as dumb as Duce? She acts like she could eat him up. Look what happened to Mike, Dasha's man, when he hung out with Duce—his crazy ass got locked up for robbing a grocery store.

Mike is doing a ten-year bid. He's already served nine years. Since Mike's been locked up, Dasha has gotten her finances together. She has worked hard to increase her salon clientele. But, she still visits Mike every weekend and she sends him big money. What's wrong with my girls?

Jaye can't stand to look at Duce any longer, so she stands up and says, "Pinkeye, I got to go." Pinkeye rolled her eyes at Jaye. She knew Jaye was leaving because Duce was there. It's no secret—Jaye does not like Duce and Duce does not like Jaye.

~

Dasha's shop was busy when Monay and Jaye walked in for their weekly appointments. "Hi Boo. I'll be with y'all after I shampoo this customer." While Jaye and Monay waited, they looked at the latest summer fashion magazines.

Jaye's favorite clothing is summer fashion. She wears all the top designer clothes. She's a creative clothing stylist and interior decorator. Jaye's mother, Mrs. Scott, opened a furniture business after Jaye graduated from college. Jaye helped her mother design the store and buy merchandise. Jaye's father passed away when she was three years old. Ever since Mrs. Scott became a widow, she has been no man's fool and she taught Jaye how to be independent.

Jaye was happy to see Dasha's shop overflowing with customers. As she looked around, admiring Dasha's thriving business, she noticed someone staring at her.

"Why is that bitch looking at me?" Jaye asked Monay.

"Oh Jaye. That's Cookie, the girl who is dating Sunny."

"Who?"

"Sunny...the guy you met at the club a while back. I heard she goes for bad."

"Well the bitch can act crazy if she wants to."

"Now Jaye, don't go starting nothing up here in Dasha's shop."

Dasha could tell by the look on Jaye's face that something was not right; and, she also saw the look that Cookie was giving Jaye. Dasha hurried and shampooed her customer and called Jaye next. Monay was glad that Dasha picked up the vibe between Jaye and Cookie. Jaye stood up and strutted pass Cookie—hoping that she would say something to her.

After Jaye and Monay finished getting their hair done, they went to Pinkeye's house. As they pulled in front of her house, a group of guys were hanging out on the corner.

"Look at them throwing their life away on booze and drugs...and they got the nerve to turn their noses up at us," said Jaye.

Chicken was standing on his porch. He lives two units down from Pinkeye. If you want to know what's going on in the hood, just ask Chicken. He is a good person at heart, but he is always running his mouth. He is a drunk, but he goes to work everyday. Chicken calls all females Squeetie, when he is really trying to say Sweetie. Chicken's sister, whose nickname is Little Bit, does not like Pinkeye. She says that Pinkeye runs a wild house and that Pinkeye looks down on her.

Last summer, Pinkeye had a barbecue at her house. Chicken stumbled over to Jaye and said, "Hey Squeetie. You sure look good. I like to get in your panties."

Jaye went off! "You drunk! You better carry your ass. Chicken you know I don't play that."

"I'm sorry Squeetie. I'm just playing with you."

"Okay, Chicken. We're still friends."

Pinkeye had the stereo blasting. Everyone was jammin' to Marvin Gaye. Little Bit banged on the front door. Pinkeye's young daughter answered the door.

"Where is that wild mother of yours?"

"Why are you banging on my mother's door like you're crazy?"

"You little fast ass—get your mother to the door!"

When Pinkeye heard Little Bit call her daughter a fast ass, she asked no questions. She punched Little Bit in the face and beat her so badly that Little Bit had to go the hospital. Since then, Little Bit has had it out for Pinkeye. And Chicken knows all about the feud between Pinkeye and his sister.

Monay and Jaye were walking up the steps to Pinkeye's front porch when Chicken came over to tell them about his sanctified crack-head sister. He told them that his sister is the biggest crack-head in the project, but she doesn't let that stop her from going to church. She's there every Sunday.

Monay heard Pinkeye talking.

"Come on Jaye. Pinkeye's fussing about something."

When Monay and Jaye walked into the house, they heard Pinkeye say before she slammed the phone down, "When I see you, I'm going to beat the brakes off of you."

"What is going on, Pinkeye?" Monay asked.

"That low budget wife of Duce keeps calling my house, calling me all kinds of names, and—she had the nerve to report me to the rent office again!"

"Since he is still with her, you need to holler at Duce about her and you need to stop fucking with Duce," Jaye said.

"I am not trying to hear that bullshit Jaye. Everyone is not like you, Miss College Graduate. You always think you know what is best for everyone—Miss Social Worker."

"What does college have to do with this? Pinkeye, you always throwing college up in my face. I'm just saying..."

Monay interrupted and quickly changed the subject. "Jaye don't say nothing. Pinkeye, we just came over to see if you wanted to go the movies tonight."

"Naw, I got a selling party going on tonight. By the way, y'all have not been to any of my card parties lately. Dasha said that she is coming when she gets off."

"We will stop by after the movies," said Monay.

"Right. Y'all some funny bitches."

Monay and Jaye left and headed to the movies. Jaye spotted Duce coming out of a crack house.

"Look at Duce! I can't stand that clown."

Duce started walking fast when he saw Monay and Jaye. Jaye made sure Duce saw them. "Hey Duce," Jaye yelled. He threw his hand up and kept walking.

"Look Monay. There goes that low budget Pea waiting for Duce so they can get high—and I bet he's buying crack with the money that Pinkeye gave him."

Pea turned her back when she saw Jaye and Monay driving down the street. "Jaye, don't say anything to Pinkeye," Monay pleaded. "What the fuck," Jaye said. "She wouldn't believe me anyway. When it comes to Duce—Pinkeye is just dumb."

~

Dasha closed up the shop after her last customer.

I need to make a doctor's appointment on Monday. All this week, I've felt dizzy and restless. Never felt like this before; I don't like it. Before I drive home, I'll call Pinkeye and let her know that I don't feel good, so I'm not coming to her party.

Dasha did not finish dialing Pinkeye's number; she passed out at the wheel of her car.

"Hi baby," said Jaye.

"How do you feel?" Monay asked.

"My head is killing me. What happened?"

"The doctor says you will be fine," Jaye said. He should be in to talk to you soon."

"How did y'all know I was in the hospital?"

"My co-worker was driving home from work and saw you slumped over in your car," Jaye told Dasha. "After calling the paramedics, she called me. Do you remember what you were doing before you passed out?"

Before Dasha could answer, a doctor walked into the room.

"Glad to see that you are awake, Miss Johnson. Ladies, will you step out of the room for a minute? I need to speak to Miss Johnson about her test results."

Jaye and Monay got up to leave. But before they could exit the room, Dasha said, "Excuse me doc, they can stay. They are like my sisters."

"Very well, Miss Johnson. You are in good health. You probably fainted due to being over fatigued. I recommend that you get more rest. You see Miss Johnson, your test results show that you are three months pregnant."

Monay and Jaye's mouths flew open.

"She is what?" Jaye whispered.

"The nurse will be in with your discharge instructions and papers." He shook Dasha's hand and left the room.

Dasha covered her face with her hands and began sobbing. "It will be all right. Don't cry," Monay said as she put her arms around Dasha.

The nurse came into the room and told Dasha that she could leave after the completion of her discharge papers. Jaye helped Dasha dress while Monay went to get the car. Dasha was quiet while Jaye was helping her.

"Do you want to talk about it?"

"Naw. There's nothing to talk about."

Monay and Jaye took Dasha home. They helped her get settled in bed. Dasha told them that she felt tired.

"Well, we will leave you for now—but we will check on you later," said Jaye.

After Monay and Jaye left, Dasha broke down and cried. Her pillow drenched with tears, she fell asleep.

On the way home, Monay and Jaye thought of Dasha and the shocking news they had just heard.

Jaye said, "I didn't know Dasha was messing around with someone."

"Jaye, don't feed into nothing."

"I was just saying that I just did not know. Let me call Pinkeye and let her know what's going on with Dasha."

"Hey Pinkeye."

"Jaye, what's up? I thought y'all was coming to my card party?"

"Girl, we just left the hospital."

"Why y'all was at the hospital?"

"Dasha was in the hospital."

"WHAT! What's wrong with her?"

"Dasha is pregnant."

"Did you say Dasha is pregnant?"

"That's right."

"How many months."

"Three."

"Get out of here. A sneaky bitch. So are y'all coming over?"

"Naw, it's too late and we're tired. Call you tomorrow."

Pinkeye went back to her party with the news about Dasha on her mind. *That's strange. Dasha usually tells me things that she would not tell Jaye and Monay. I know the last time she was over my house, she ate like a pig. I never gave it any thought. Now if Mike is in jail, who in the hell could she be pregnant by.*

"Hey! Put my chair back in the corner where you found it," shouted Pinkeye. "You niggurs be getting on my nerves, always messing with shit that's not yours."

Chicken, with a 12 pack of beer, knocked on Pinkeye's door. "Hey Squeetie. Can I come to your selling party?"

"Come in. But I am not going to have any problems out of you Chicken. You got that?"

"Yes Squeetie."

"Pump the music back up!" Pinkeye shouted. The party came alive again. Chicken was glad that Pinkeye let him in. He walked around smiling in everyone's face.

Pinkeye announced that the party would be over in an hour. "Y'all niggurs got to get up out of here."

~

After dropping off Monay, Jaye decided to call Jackson and invite him over.

Jackson gives Jaye whatever she wants and Jaye really doesn't treat Jackson right. Jaye has it all—good looks, shapely body, good job, and men on the side. Jackson is too slow for her. Jaye likes fast men and—fast money.

As soon as Jaye walked in her house, she picked up the phone to call Jackson—someone knocked on her door. With the phone in her hand, she answered the door. It was Jackson.

"What's up baby?"

"I was just going to call you."

Jackson laughed, "The only time you call me is when you want something."

"Oh come on Jackson. You know I be calling you, but you are never home."

"Save it Jaye. My boy told me he saw you out at the club with low rider jeans on and that the fellows were really checking you out."

"Your boys are the main ones lookin'. Don't come in here like we married and stuff." Jaye always won when they argued.

"Jackson, you be letting them, who you call your boys, hit you in the head with a lot of dumb stuff. I don't have time for this foolishness."

She walked in her bedroom and sat on the bed.

He came behind her, "Jaye, you know I love you."

"Jackson, I don't like it when you be running tabs on me."

"I'm not running tabs on you, baby. Here—take this." Jackson gave her five hundred dollars.

Jaye tried to look mad, but deep down inside she was happy as hell.

~

After a restless night, Monay lay in bed wondering why she hadn't heard from Maleake. All kinds of thoughts were going through her head.

Why does Maleake always lie to me? Maybe I'm not doing my part. I need to buy him a few summer designer outfits. I'm sure that will make him feel better about being with me.

Monay reached for her phone. She paged Maleake. Ten minutes later, he called.

"What's up, baby?"

"Maleake, I haven't heard from you in a week."

"I know baby, I've been job hunting so I can take you on a cruise this summer."

"Oh Maleake. I love you so much. Why don't you come over this evening and I'll fix a nice dinner."

"True that baby. I will be there around seven."

Maleake hung up the phone. *I got that dumb bitch going. I'll go over her house for dinner and some—and then after that— I'll tell her that I've got somewhere to go.*

~

Before Pinkeye went to bed, she cleaned up the mess from her selling party. *The next time I throw a party, I'm going to make sure I get them niggurs to help me clean up before they leave.*

Pinkeye went outside to dump the trash. She saw Little Bit coming down the street after scoring from the crack house. Little Bit tried to act like she didn't see Pinkeye.

"Hey Miss Sanctified Crack Head. Thought you could get by me?" Pinkeye hollered.

Little Bit gave Pinkeye the finger and started running. Pinkeye tossed her trash bag and chased after Little Bit.

"Oh, I'll see your crack head ass again," Pinkeye shouted as Little Bit ran in the house.

Pinkeye dumped her trash, went back into her house and finished cleaning.

Later, she sat down and counted the money she had made from her party. She was pleased with her profit. She made enough money to buy the school clothes that she'd promised her daughters. Before falling asleep, she put her money in a bama box on her bedside table.

An hour later, Duce came into the house and called out for Pinkeye. No answer.

Duce knew Pinkeye had made good money from her selling party. He walked in the bedroom and saw Pinkeye knocked out—asleep. He also saw Pinkeye's bama box. Duce took Pinkeye's money out of the box and left.

Duce knew he was wrong— but like always, he knew that Pinkeye would be mad for a few days, but that she would soon forgive him. Duce headed to the crack house and spent every dime.

~

Dasha woke up after a long hard cry. She felt tired and was hungry as hell. As she tried to energize herself with a few stretches, her phone rang.

"Hello."

"Hey Dasha, how are you feeling?"

"I'm fine."

"Do you want to go out for breakfast this morning?" Jaye asked.

"Why not."

"I'm starving Dasha. I'll be over to pick you up around ten o'clock."

Jaye hoped that Dasha would talk about her pregnancy and tell her who—is the baby's daddy. *I will let her do the talking; I will just listen.*

Dasha got dressed and waited for Jaye to pick her up. She thought about what the doctor said—*Miss Johnson, you are three months pregnant.*

As she paced back and forth thinking about her situation, the sound of the doorbell startled her.

"Girl, open this damn door...taking your time like your mind is bad," Jaye shouted.

Dasha laughed and opened the door.

"Hey Boo. You ready?"

"Yes, let me get my bag."

"Oh no! Naw. You ain't carrying a Louis Vuitton?"

"I bought it from Macy's last week."

"You go girl. That's what's up!"

~

Monay looked at her watch. She only had three hours to shop; then she had to rush home and cook a five star meal for Maleake.

Riding down the street, she popped in a Fifty Cent's CD. *That's my song—Shake, shake, shake your ass girl put your back into it. I know that's right. I will be doing just that to Maleake in about five more hours.*

Monay arrived at the mall and spotted a parking space. She saw a black BMW going for the same space. She blew her horn and shouted, "I was here first!"

"It's okay," said the gentleman, "ladies first."

"You got that right." Monay parked and grabbed her Gucci bag. As she was getting out of her car, she saw the person who she honked at for the parking space—*Well catch me ground. What a man! What a man!* Before she walked away from her car, Monay made sure her Azzure jeans and top were in place.

Monay has a cute shape and good looks with hazel eyes and full lips. She is medium brown with a nice grade of hair that she wears in a dubby wrap.

"Hello."

"Hi."

"You look like you're in a hurry," he said as he gave Monay his business card. "My name is James. Maybe we can have dinner some day."

"Now why should I do that? I just met you. You don't even know my name."

"I'm sorry. What is your name shorty?"

"Monay."

"That's a nice name."

"Thank you. Well I got to go."

Monay did not look at his card. She just threw it in her purse and headed toward the front door of the mall. James smiled as he watched Monay's tight buttocks sway from side to side. *I hope she calls.*

Monay went from store to store buying gifts for Maleake. She purchased quite a few latest summer fashions and colognes. All she wanted was to please Maleake in every way.

~

Jaye treated Dasha to breakfast at I-HOP. "Slow down girl, before you bust your belly open," Jaye said as she watched Dasha eat like a pig.

Dasha wanted to laugh but her mouth was too full.

"Well Miss Dasha, how are things coming along at the shop?"

"Girl, the shop is doing good. My regulars passed out my new business cards and that brought in new customers. I'm thinking about remodeling."

"That would be nice," said Jaye. "Let me know if you need any help."

Jaye's phone rang.

"Hello."

"Hello Jaye," said Jackson.

"Hi Jackson. What's up?"

"Jaye, I wanted to know if you would like to go to New York?"

"When?"

"Next weekend. I have some new arrivals coming in and I would like you to help me pick out my fall fashions."

"Sure. I'd love to."

Jackson owns four men's clothing stores with top-of-the-line fashions. Jaye likes Jackson because he buys her expensive gifts and gives her lots of money.

As soon as Jaye hung up, she started telling Dasha all about what Jackson had just told her.

"Hey girl. Where is your head? I'm talking to you and you look like you've lost your best friend."

"What you say, Jaye?"

"Nothing Dasha. Let's go to the mall."

~

A discussion about buying school clothes escalated into an argument; the screaming and shouting woke up Pinkeye.

"I'm trying to sleep," Pinkeye shouted at her daughters. "Y'all shut the hell up before I come in there and knock some ass off."

The house got quiet.

It was almost noon, so Pinkeye decided to get up and start cooking her food for tomorrow. She always liked to cook her Sunday dinner on Saturday. She'd tell her girls—*Food taste better after the seasoning settles in for a day.* Eating Sunday dinner at Pinkeye's was like eating at a down-home soul food restaurant. There was always a lot of food, including homemade rolls.

Pinkeye made her bed and tidied up her bedroom. She thought about the money she made at her party last night. Her profit was more than she'd expected. She wasn't comfortable about keeping that much money in her house so she thought about asking Monay to keep it in her home safe.

As she dusted her bedside table, Pinkeye knocked over her bama box. It fell open on the floor—the box was empty—her money was gone!

Pinkeye screamed!

"That damned Duce came in my house and beat me for my money. I know he took my money, because my children would never take anything from me without asking first," Pinkeye shouted. She hurried and showered, got dressed, and went down the street—looking for Duce.

Pinkeye walked up to Pea who was standing in front of the crack house, "Where is Duce?"

"I have not seen him."

Pinkeye knew Pea was lying. "If I find out that you lied to me, I'm going to beat the brakes off your ass."

Pea was always scared of Pinkeye so she decided to tell on Duce. "Pinkeye, I saw Duce about an hour ago, spending money like his mind was bad."

"Oh, is that right," said Pinkeye. "Well if you see him again, tell him I'm going to fuck his ass up."

What Pea didn't tell Pinkeye was that she helped Duce spend the money on crack.

~

Jaye and Dasha arrived at the mall. The parking lot was full. While driving around looking for a space, they spotted Monay's car. "That's why I could not reach Monay before I picked you up," Jaye told Dasha. She parked in the same row that Monay was parked.

"I'll park here. This way, if we don't see Monay inside the mall, hopefully she will see my car and know that we are here."

Dasha got out of the car and walked around to Jaye's side. She started feeling dizzy. Dasha vomited and stumbled backwards. Jaye caught Dasha and helped her back into the car. Dasha sat for about 15 minutes while Jaye wiped her forehead.

"I feel better now."

"Do you throw up like this all the time?"

"No, this is my first time."

Ladies' Night

As soon as Jaye and Dasha walked into the mall, they smelled fresh popcorn. Jaye said, "Oh that smells good. I must get me a bag before I leave." "Don't leave me out!" Dasha replied.

"Look Jaye, there goes Monay. Damn! Looks like she bought half of the mall."

"Mo!" Jaye called out.

Oh no! That's the last person I need to see. I know she is going to say something about all my shopping bags.

"Hi ladies," Monay said. "What y'all doing here?"

"Oh, we went out to breakfast. I tried to call you, but your answering machine came on. I didn't leave a message. Monay, what do you have planned for tonight?" Jaye asked. "I was hoping we could all get together and go to the club."

"Well, Maleake is coming over for dinner," said Monay.

"Count me out too," said Dasha. I'm going to relax and look at some videos that I rented."

"Well," said Jaye, "I guess I'll go by myself and have a few drinks and listen to a little music."

Jaye looked down at the bags Monay was carrying. *She really hooked Maleake up this time. I know Monay spent about a thousand dollars on all of that stuff.*

When Monay saw Jaye looking at her bags, she started moving around like she was ready to go.

"Hey, why don't we all meet at church," Monay said.

"Okay," said Jaye and Dasha.

"I'll give Pinkeye a call and see if she wants to join us."

"You know Pinkeye isn't trying to go to church," said Dasha.

"Well, I'll see y'all later." Monay hugged Jaye and Dasha and left.

"Monay is my girl, but she is dumb. Dasha, I know she worked overtime so that she could buy Maleake those outfits. Did you see the look on her face when she saw us? I thought she was going to faint."

Jaye stopped talking to look at her caller ID.

"Now what does this niggur want. I have not heard from him in two months," Jaye said as she put her cell phone back into her purse. "You know Dasha, some calls just don't need to be answered."

Jaye and Dasha went into Macy's. Dasha saw a pair of shoes that she liked and bought them. Jaye fell in love with a bad Armani jumpsuit. She tried it on and admired herself in the mirror.

A little girl who was waiting outside of the dressing room for her mother looked at Jaye and said, "You look pretty."

Jaye bent down and smiled at the little girl. As she and the little girl were talking, two thugs walked up and admired Jaye.

"Girl, you sure make a niggur holler."

"Show some respect. This is my daughter. Besides, if you were real men, you would already know how to respect ladies and give a lady a compliment."

"No problem baby girl," said one of the guys.

"Well, keep it moving. Just keep it moving!" Jaye yelled.

Dasha walked over to the baby's section and started looking at all the beautiful baby clothes and furniture. She thought about her dreams of being married before having a child— Mike's child. She and Mike had talked about getting married first, and then having children. A sales lady interrupted Dasha's thoughts. "May I help you?" "No," said Dasha, "I was just looking."

Dasha hurried out of the baby's department. Jaye saw Dasha walking around like she was in a daze. "I'm over here, girl," Jaye yelled.

"That jumpsuit looks good on you," said Dasha.

"I need to find a pair of shoes to go with it." Jaye's cell phone rang again. "Damn this phone." She answers. "What's up?"

"Nothing Miss Jaye. I was just calling to ask you out to dinner tonight."

"Now that's what's up. Pick me up around seven," Jaye said before she hung up. After Jaye found shoes to match her jumpsuit, she and Dasha bought popcorn and left the mall.

~

Pinkeye couldn't find Duce. She returned home, mad as hell! The phone was ringing when she walked into the house.

"Hello."

It was Dasha. "Hey Pinkeye, what's up?"

"Girl, Duce came in here this morning and stole the money that I made from my selling party."

"What! How much did he take?"

"Six hundred fifty dollars. You know when I see Duce, it's on. He can't tell me a damn thing."

"I'm sorry to hear that. I was calling to see if you wanted to go to church with us tomorrow?"

"Girl, I ain't going to no church."

"That will lift you up."

"The only thing that will lift me is my foot up Duce's ass."

"Maybe I'll come by after church."

"Do that. I'll have dinner finished when you get here. Ask Jaye and Monay if they would like to come."

"I was with Jaye today," Dasha said.

"I thought y'all were coming by tonight."

"Jaye got a phone call from one of her players, so she's going out tonight and Monay is having dinner with Maleake," Dasha explained to Pinkeye. "I am going to relax and watch movies. We will see you tomorrow."

~

Dasha was watching a movie when her phone rang. "Hello."

"Hey baby, what's up? I haven't heard from you in two weeks."

"Oh, hi Mike. What's up with you?"

"What's up with the—oh hi Mike?"

"Nothing. I was just watching a movie. Did you get the money that I sent you?"

"Baby, I got the money but I want to see you. Why haven't you been to see me?"

"I've been busy at the shop. I'll come next Saturday after my last customer."

The operator interrupted the call with a two-minute warning that the call would end. Mike told Dasha to send him a pair of Nike's and two pairs of jeans. The phone disconnected. Dasha stared at the phone.

What the hell am I going to do? Mike has seven months left in jail and I am pregnant.

~

Monay had the table set and soft jazz playing. Everything was ready—a great dinner with Maleake's favorite foods and a sexy teddy that she would wear after dinner. She neatly placed on her bed, his new outfits that cost—more than eight hundred dollars. All she wanted was for Maleake to have the time of his life, spending it with her—just her.

Monay's phone rang.

"Hello."

"Hey Mo. What's up? Have you fixed dinner for Maleake yet?" Jaye asked.

"Girl, I cooked a dinner that Maleake is going to enjoy."

"Whatever you cooked, I know it's great. I just hope he appreciates it. You know Maleake always knows how to win you over."

"Jaye, don't start it with me. What I do for Maleake is my business and no one—has anything to do with it."

"Monay, I'm just looking out."

"Thanks Jaye, but I'm okay."

"Well have a good dinner and I'll see you in church tomorrow."

~

Jaye took a shower, got dressed and admired herself in the mirror. *Damn, you look good.*

Oh! I forgot to call Mom. I told her that I would call her when I got home. Jaye picked up the phone and dialed her mom's number.

"Hey Mom."

"Jaye, where have you been?"

"Dasha and I hung out at the mall all day. Oh, by the way Mom, Dasha's pregnant."

"PREGNANT! I thought her boyfriend was in jail."

"He is Mom."

"Then who is she pregnant by?"

"I don't know."

"Jaye, where are you going tonight?"

"I'm going out with a friend."

"Someone I know?"

"No Mom, It's no one you know."

"Jaye, you need to stay focused on Jackson. He's the one for you. It's hard to find a good man like Jackson."

"Mom, I'm not in love with Jackson."

"Jaye, don't miss your blessing."

"Mom, I've got to go. My date is at the door."

No one was at the door but Jaye told her mother that to end the conversation. She thought about how her mother has always liked Jackson.

Mom is always telling me to marry Jackson and give her some grandchildren—yeah right. I know she's tripping. One thing's for sure, Jackson kicks that money out when I need it.

~

Pinkeye sat up most of the night thinking about how she was going to get the money for her daughters' school clothes. She heard a knock at the front door. It was Harold.

"Hey Pinkeye. Let me in girl!"

"Where have you been?" Pinkeye asked.

"I've been around."

"Yeah, digging in Pea's trick ass. I know you thought that I didn't know that you have been trickin' with her."

"Now come on Pinkeye. I don't say nothin' when you see Duce."

"I know one thing. You messing around with that old trick ass bitch and you think I'm going to lay up with you. I don't think so."

"Come on Pinkeye," Harold pleaded. "You know I'll look out for you."

"Harold, keep it moving unless you can help me get my girls' school clothes."

"Pinkeye, I won't have any money until next week."

"Then, I'll see you next week."

"Girl, you drive a hard bargain."

"Carry your broke ass!"

Harold gave Pinkeye twenty dollars for her girls and left.

Pinkeye slid the twenty down in her bust line. *I can't believe Duce took my money. He can't tell me nothing this time. If he doesn't have my money, this relationship is over.*

She slipped on her oven mitts. *Those bitches better come for dinner tomorrow or they won't have another Sunday meal at this house.*

~

Monay got dressed. She looked around to make sure that everything was in place. She saw Maleake pull into her driveway. "Oh, he's driving his sister's car."

Maleake has never owned a car. He always drives one of his women's car or his sister's car.

Monay, with all smiles, opened the door.

"Hey Baby Girl," Maleake said, "You sure know how to hook things up."

"Come here Maleake," Monay said as she took him into her bedroom, "I have a surprise for you." She showed him the clothes that she bought him.

Maleake checked out his silk shirts, dressed pants, jeans, hats, and underclothes. *Damn, that bitch will do anything for me. I know I got to do some extra shit to her tonight.*

He grabbed Monay's head and kissed her all over her face.

Monay could feel her clitoris getting moist and wanted Maleake then and there. He whispered in her ear, "in due time, in due time". Monay let go and gently kissed his lips before walking out of the bedroom.

Maleake looked at his watch and thought about where he had to be in a few hours. He had something going on with one of his other ladies, who he is really into. Unlike Monay, this woman takes no shit from Maleake.

"Baby let's eat," he said.

Monay fixed their plates—T-bone steak, jumbo shrimp, baked potato, and Caesar salad. Then she poured him a glass of expensive wine. After eating a sumptuous dinner, Maleake went into the living room and lay on the sofa, feeling damn good.

Before going into her bedroom to slip on a sexy teddy, Monay dimmed the living room lights. When she quietly walked back into the living room, she put on a Boney James CD—then she walked over to Maleake and gently pressed her fingers against his lips.

Maleake opened his eyes and pulled Monay on top of him. While squeezing her ass, he slid his tongue up and down her breast. Monay could not take it anymore.

"Oh Maleake, I want you inside of me. Please! Please!" She begged.

Maleake took Monay to her bedroom. The soft sounds of Bony James continued to play as Maleake began to spread Monay's legs apart. He entered slowly inside her moist clit. She screamed to the top of her voice, crying out, "I love you, I love you." Maleake could no longer hold back. They both exploded uncontrollably and held on tight to each other.

Maleake lay there thinking about going to see his other woman.

"Hey baby, I got something I need to take care of. I'll be back in an hour."

"I thought you were going to stay all night and have breakfast with me?"

"Baby, this is important business that I need to take care of."

He took a quick shower, got dressed, and bagged up his new clothes.

"Why are you taking your clothes if you are planning on coming back?" Monay asked.

"I need to hang 'em up so they won't get wrinkled."

"Oh well, hurry and come back."

Maleake got in the car and smiled all the time while he was driving. *I've got Monay on lock down. She'll give me what I want—whenever I want it.*

Counting the Days

Mike walked around his jail cell wondering why Dasha hadn't been to see him. He was depending on Dasha to take care of him when he got out. He planned to get a part-time job and hustle at night. The job was to impress his probation officer and the judge.

Damn. I've got another woman that would look out for me, but Dasha makes good money and I know that I can get back on my feet in no time with her. She's always talking about getting married and having a baby. I don't know about getting married, but I'd love to give Dasha a baby. Marriage is out of the picture. I'm not trying to be tied down with a family. I've been locked up for nine years—I got things to do.

"Lights out," shouted one of the prison guards.

While staring at a dull beam of light through his cell bars, Mike thought about what he was going to do when he got out. He was sure that Dasha would make him co-owner of her business. *After I make bank for a year, I will never have to work again and my hustling days will be history.*

~

Jaye's date took her home with high hopes that she would invite him in.

Oh no he doesn't think he's coming in for a booty-call. He got what he paid for, and what he paid really wasn't enough. This was a waste of my time.

"Are you going to invite me in?"

"I got to get up early and do something for my mom."

"Can I catch up with you next week?"

"Next weekend I'll be out of town on a business trip. Good night."

Jaye closed her front door and immediately went to check her messages. Jackson had called eight times and she had so many other calls from her players that the answering machine battery weakened.

Jaye could not wait to call Jackson. That was the only call that she wanted to return. Her other players would have to wait until tomorrow or maybe next week.

I know I got to hit Jackson back. That's my money and that clown-toy that I was out with tonight watches every dime he spends—old coupon-type niggur. I know I got to keep it moving and do not answer my phone when he calls again. He's nice, but nice don't pay the bills.

"Hey baby. I noticed you called eight times." Jaye tried to sound like she had been sleeping. "Is there something wrong?"

"No, I was just calling to see if you wanted to go out for drinks."

"Jackson, I was tired when I got home from work. I'd planned to take a nap, but slept longer and I just woke up. Baby, I'll see you tomorrow. Okay?"

"I love you, Jaye."

"Same here."

Jaye hated for Jackson to say that he loved her. That put her on the spot to say she loved him back.

She took a shower and went to bed.

~

Dasha woke up late. "Damn, I have a customer scheduled for 8:00 and it's already 7:45." She jumped out of bed, took a shower, and got dressed. In less than 20 minutes, Dasha was at her shop. She was shocked to see so many customers waiting.

Dasha apologized for being late, opened her shop, and started setting up for her day. But within minutes, she started feeling queasy. Dasha asked her customers to give her five minutes; then she went into the bathroom and vomited. When she came out of the bathroom, many customers were staring at her. *I know they are wondering what is wrong with me.*

As soon as she started shampooing her first customer, the shop's phone rang. Apologizing again, Dasha stopped and answered the phone. It was Pinkeye.

"What is this shit that you are pregnant?"

"Yes, Pinkeye. I am."

Before Pinkeye could ask another question, Dasha said, "Pinkeye someone is beeping in my line. I will see you Sunday."

"Cut me off like that, huh. Okay. I'll talk to you later."

~

Duce better not come in here talking shit today. I know he took my money, but that's okay. I got a trick for his ass.

Pinkeye put her dinner on the stove and sat down to think things over. She wondered why Duce would take her money. Maybe he needed the money to buy food for his kids. But even if that was the reason, she did not understand why he had to take all of her money.

Now, I've got to try and get the money back to buy my children's school clothes.

Pinkeye thought long and hard about how she could make some money before school opened. She decided that the quickest way was—to have another selling party, and this time she would ask Monay, Dasha, and Jaye to help her. She knew Jaye would object to her idea.

~

Monay stared out of the window knowing, by now, that Maleake was not coming back. Her eyes filled with tears, she called him four times on his cell phone, but he did not answer.

He knows that we planned to eat breakfast together. What was so important that he had to leave like that? Jaye tells me that Maleake is making a fool out of me. How can she talk— when she is making a fool out of Jackson. I hope Maleake calls me in the morning.

Monay feels that she gives Maleake all that he needs, so he has no reason to be with another woman. She loves him and vows to do anything for him, but she is beginning to get suspicious.

As Monay slid between her sheets, she thought about the passion she felt when Maleake made love to her. But now, she feels alone; she calls Pinkeye.

"Hey Pinkeye. This is Mo. I'm calling to see if you want me to bring something for dinner?"

"Bring sodas and tell Jaye and Dasha to bring dessert. Oh by the way, what do you think about Dasha having a baby? Do you think she's been giving Mike some?"

"I don't think so. You got to be married before the prison will give you a private room to do that."

"Well, I sure would like to know who's the baby's daddy."

"Pinkeye, please don't ask her. You know how she gets."

"Monay, I'm not thinking about that swamp coochie."

"Girl, you wild. It would take you to say something like that. Let me call Dasha and Jaye. Oh, I forgot Jaye is out on a date."

"I thought you were having dinner with Maleake?"

"Oh we had dinner—and Pinkeye, the niggur gave it to me like I never had it before."

"You go girl. I wish Duce would give me the wood like that. Naw! His ass so busy in the streets."

Pinkeye did not want to tell Monay about Duce taking her money.

"I'm going to finish cooking. I'll see you tomorrow. Peace."

~

Dasha's feet were hurting after standing for ten hours. She ran water in the bathtub to take a relaxing bath. Before the tub filled, the phone rang. "Hello." It was Monay.

"Hey Dasha. I am not going to talk long. I talked to Pinkeye about dinner tomorrow. I'm bringing sodas and she asked me to tell you and Jaye to bring dessert."

"Okay," said Dasha. "I will let Jaye know. I am getting ready to soak my feet—they are killing me. I'll see you tomorrow."

Dasha filled her foot massager with a foot softener, slid her feet into the warm water, and relaxed. She jumped.

Oh, what was that! She could see a knot in her stomach, but when she rubbed her stomach, it went away.

After soaking her feet, she got in the tub and dozed for about five minutes. She felt so relaxed. She woke up and ran more hot water in the bathtub.

Dasha bathed, got out of the tub, and wrapped herself in a downing fresh smelling towel. After lying on the bed and thinking about her baby, she rubbed down with a Victoria Secret lotion. Dasha got in bed and took no time to fall asleep.

When she first heard the phone ring, she thought she was dreaming. She opened her eyes and looked at her clock. *Who could be calling me this time of the night?*

"Hello."

"You have a collect call from Serville Prison. Will you accept the call?" Asked the operator.

"Yes," said Dasha.

"Where the hell your ass been all day?" Mike asked.

Dasha told Mike that she had been working and that she had a lot of walk-ins at the shop. She tried to tell him how tired she was from working long hours but Mike didn't want to hear it.

"Don't give me that bullshit. I been calling your cell phone and the shop. Did you send me the money I asked for last week? You need to come and holler at me."

"I sent the money yesterday. Mike, I have a lot on me. I'm trying to find a contractor that will not charge much to remodel my shop."

"I did not ask you that," said Mike. "When are you coming up here?"

"I will be there next week. My schedule is not that heavy."

The operator cut into the line. Dasha was glad to hear that it was time to end the call.

"That's my time," said Mike, "I will call you before the week is out."

Dasha said goodbye and went back to sleep.

~

Jaye slept all day and most of the night. When she woke up, it was 9:30 p.m. *Damn I told Mom that I would help her today. I know she is going to lay me out. I will call her after I eat.*

She looked at her caller ID and saw that she had ten calls. While she ate, Jaye listened to her messages. Monay called about Sunday dinner at Pinkeye's and Jackson left several messages for her to call him back. *I'm long overdue. I guess I will give Jackson some play. I know he is going to kick out some coins before he leaves.*

She called Jackson on his cell phone.

"Hey baby," said Jackson, "Having company tonight?"

"Come on over," Jaye said.

"Well, I'll see you in an hour."

She took a hot bath and called her mother when she got out of the tub.

"Hi Mom."

"Jaye I called you several times on both your house and cell phones."

"Ma, I was so tired. I've been going to court every day this week—making home visits, and moving children around in different foster homes."

"Jaye you need to work on getting your boys' group home and going back to school to get your Masters."

"Ma, I'm going back to school next semester. I've already submitted my papers to the Master of Social Work program at Norfolk State."

"Good for you," said her mother. "Well listen, I need you to come over here tomorrow and help me rearrange my living room furniture."

"Ma, I'm going to church and then to Pinkeye's for dinner. I'll be over after dinner."

"Jaye, are you going to our church?"

"Naw. I'm going to Dasha's church."

"That's nice. I know Pinkeye is cooking rolls. Tell her to send me some. Is she going to church?"

"Ma, you know Pinkeye is not going to church."

Hard Times Ahead

Pinkeye stayed up most of the night cooking her Sunday dinner. All she could think about was how she was going to make money at her next selling party.

The phone rang and broke her concentration. *Who in the hell is calling my house this time of the morning?*

"Hello," she answered while fixing her mouth to curse the person out on the other end.

"Hey Boo, what's up?" It was Duce.

"You know what's up," said Pinkeye. "You stole the money that I made from my selling party."

"You say what?"

"Duce don't come with that at me."

"What you talking about, Boo?"

"Before I fell asleep, I put my money in a bama box on my bedside table. Your monkey ass took it while I was sleeping."

"You know I wouldn't take anything from you."

"You can carry that shit, Duce. My children would not take from me and your monkey ass is the only other person who walks freely in my house."

"Pinkeye, I came to your house and brought Pea with me to see if you wanted to buy some hot clothes for your girls. I called out your name twice. I went to the bathroom and left Pea in the living room. She must have gone into your bedroom and looked in the box and took your money."

"What! You had that swamp coochie bitch in my house. When I see that Pea, I'm going to bust that bitch's head to the white meat. And by the way, where your ass been?"

"I rode with a friend to Richmond."

"Duce you are a damn lie. Chicken told me that he saw you on the corner yesterday with Pea."

"That drunk don't know what he is talking about and when I see him I'm going to fuck his ass up."

"Duce, you not going to do a damn thing to Chicken. You must think I'm crazy. Chicken might be a drunk, but he's no liar. He will tell on his own mother."

"So you putting Chicken's word before me?"

"You are a stupid ass man. What the hell I want with Chicken?"

"You know what—I have done a lot of things, but to take from your children, I could never do that Pinkeye."

"Duce, that time when you took my rent money—you didn't think about my children then. You tell Pea that she'd better watch her back.

And by the way, I need for you to come over my house and help me get stuff down from the closets. I'm having dinner for my friends."

"I can do that," said Duce. "I'll be there early. Peace."

Pinkeye thought about how strangely Pea acted when she asked her about Duce.

Pea lied to me. That's okay. Wait until I see her.

With her money gone, Pinkeye was so upset that she sat on the side of her bed and dozed off. After a couple of hours, she woke up and sat by her bedroom window. Pinkeye saw Chicken coming down the street. She raised the window and hollered.

"Hey Chicken. Let me talk at you for a minute. Check it out. I'm planning another selling party next weekend."

"Now that's what's up," said Chicken. "You throw live parties Pinkeye, but your drinks is higher than gas."

"Fuck you Chicken. Y'all broke ass niggurs give your money for that cheap beer and wine to them damn foreigners on the corner. Their prices are higher than the good liquor I be selling. I tell you what Chicken, you keep your black ass home."

"Now, now Squeetie. Why you trying to carry like that? I'll be there."

"Well stop talking out the side of your neck, Chicken. I'll holler at you later."

~

Monay woke up and called Maleake. Six times, she dialed his number, but he never answered. *He lied again. Why do I put up with this shit? Maybe I love him too much.*

Feeling the need to talk to one of her girls, she called Dasha.

"Hello."

"Hey girl," said Monay.

"Hi," said Dasha.

"Why are you talking so low?" Monay asked.

"Girl, I thought you were Mike. He's been calling here since yesterday."

"Why don't you want to talk to him?"

"I don't feel like talking to him. Besides, I'll be going to visit him next week."

"So how are you doing little Mommy?"

"I'm doing fine. I just feel a little sick when I first get up in the morning."

"Girl, Maleake was supposed to come back to my house last night. I have not heard a word from him."

"Wait a minute Dasha. Someone is beeping in."

"Hello."

"Hi baby."

"Hi Maleake. I thought you were coming back last night."

"Baby, I got caught up, but I will see you later on today."

"Maleake, I'm going over to Pinkeye's house for dinner. Why don't you come to my house about 6:00 this evening?"

"That's a bet. Peace."

"I'm back, Dasha. That was Maleake. He's coming over here after I get home from Pinkeye's."

"Girl, let me get off this phone and get dressed for church."

~

Mike looked at his watch for what seemed like the one-hundredth time. He knew Dasha was avoiding his calls. With only seven months left in prison, he was getting anxious as he anticipated what would happen when he got out. Mike was determined that he was going to rule Dasha.

He took out his money book. *For eight years, I have saved most of the money that Dasha sent me.*

He thought about how Dasha had faithfully sent him money every week. But he felt that something was not right because she had not visited him in two weeks. *That bitch better tell me why she has not been up here lately.*

Mike was thinking all kinds of crazy thoughts.

I know one thing that bitch better keep it real with me. If I find out she's fucking with another niggur, she is going to regret that. So what if I've been locked up for nine years.

Then again, that educated bitch, Jaye, might be putting shit about me in Dasha's head. Jaye's always running her motherfucking mouth. If she was my woman, I'd been done beat her ass.

Mike thought back to the time when Dasha caught him in her bed with another woman.

Dasha went off. I beat her ass right there in her own bedroom. The other girl got her ass up and went in the living room. I never heard another word about it from neither one of them. I control my women—and I'm damn good at it!

Mike has a bad habit of beating women when they don't do what he demands. One time he hit Dasha in the head with his fist when she would not give him any money. Ever since that incident, Dasha does what Mike tells her to do.

~

I know Pinkeye is calling me all kind of nasty names. I better get around to her house right now. Duce was making his way to Pinkeye's house, when he saw Chicken down the street.

"Chicken, let me holler at you?"

"What's up Duce?"

"Chicken man, you told Pinkeye that you saw me standing on the corner the other day spending money like my mind was bad."

Before Chicken could say anything, Duce slammed Chicken in the face and Chicken hit the ground hard. A crowd gathered around and everyone was asking Duce why he hit Chicken like that.

All of a sudden Chicken's sister, Little Bit, pushed her way through the crowd and hit Duce with a stick. When she saw her brother's face bleeding, she lost it; she kept hitting Duce over and over again—until he was unconscious.

Someone from the crowd shouted, "Beat that grease niggur to sleep!" "Knock the hell out of his grease ass," another person shouted.

Ten minutes later, you could hear the sirens—police and ambulance—headed for the projects again. People scattered and ran. Duce lay on the ground in a pool of blood.

Duce has a reputation, in the hood, of beating up people for their money. Then after he beats them, he turns around and talks shit. He has more haters than friends.

Chicken got up and ran behind his sister. The police officers were trying to get information about what happened but no one said a word.

Duce was rushed to the hospital.

~

Jackson sat at his desk thinking about his upcoming activities for the next few months. He thought about proposing to Jaye. *She is the only woman that I want. I love her so much. I will do anything for Jaye.*

Jackson thought about Jaye having his children. He loved children and cherished the thought of Jaye being the mother of his children.

His serene thoughts were interrupted when his secretary walked in to discuss making reservations for his New York trip. Jackson told her that he would take care of it. Since Jaye was going to New York with him, he wanted to make all the plans. Jackson always kept his personal life separate from his business affairs.

The next day Jackson made all of the New York arrangements for two—including dinner reservations at an upscale restaurant. After he completed his business in New York, he planned to take Jaye shopping and let her buy whatever she wanted.

Jackson looked at his Rolex watch. He could not wait to be with Jaye tonight.

Jackson is a well-groomed man and wears the best designer clothes that any man would love to wear. Two years ago, he bought a three-story condo in the Ocean View area of Norfolk. He can have any woman he wants, but his heart belongs to Jaye.

~

Monay picked up the phone to call Dasha. The phone rang five times before she answered.

"Hello."

"Girl what took you so long to answer the phone?" Monay asked.

"I was trying to zip up my dress. My stomach has gotten big."

"Dasha you need to start buying maternity clothes."

"I agree. Next week, Jaye and I are going shopping. I'll buy some maternity outfits then."

"Well get dressed. I am on my way to pick you up and then we will pick up Jaye."

Everything Dasha tried on was too tight. She looked in the mirror, turning side to side. She agreed with Monay. Her stomach was getting too big for her clothes. She looked in her closet and selected a jumpsuit that had an elastic waistband. She put the suit on and it felt better over her stomach. Even though she had gained weight, she looked good in the suit and she knew it. Her makeup was hooked. Dasha felt good about herself.

Dasha heard Monay honking her horn. She grabbed her purse and was headed out the door when the phone rang.

She went back into the house and answered the phone.

"Hello."

"Don't hello me." It was Mike, who had managed to call without going through an operator.

"Mike, I'm on my way to church."

"You are not going nowhere. Sit down and let me tell you what I want you to know. I am tired of your bullshit. What the hell you take me for—a damn fool?"

"Mike, Monay is waiting for me outside."

"Tell her you ain't going nowhere."

"Mike call me tonight."

"What the hell did I just hear you say?"

Monay continued to honk her horn. Between Mike screaming at her on the phone and Monay honking her car horn, Dasha began feeling agitated. She could not take it anymore. She closed her eyes and asked the Lord to guide her through this; then she hung up the phone without saying goodbye and walked out of her house.

Dasha had tears in her eyes when she got into Monay's car.

"Why are you crying?" Monay asked.

"Mike just called. He was yelling on the phone—telling me what I better do—like I am a child."

"Dasha, don't let Mike upset you—especially now that you are pregnant."

~

Monay's phone rang. It was Maleake.

"Hey baby."

"Are you still coming over my house?" Monay asked.

"Yes. Baby check this out. I need five hundred dollars to buy a car that I saw today at Charles Auto."

"Sure. I will let the money be your Christmas gift."

"Thanks baby, I'll see you later."

Monay hung up and was all smiles. She looked in her rear view mirror and admired how her makeup looked. Dasha looked at Monay and asked if that was Maleake who just called.

"Yes. Why you ask?"

"Oh, I just wanted to say hello."

What Dasha really wanted to tell Monay was—don't give him any more money.

"Oh, I forgot to call Jaye," Monay said as her phone rang.

It was Jaye. "Girl I was just getting ready to call you."

"We must have been thinking, at the same time, about calling each other," said Jaye. "I was just calling to tell you not to come by because I am driving my car today. After dinner, I have to go to my mother's house. I'm leaving for church now."

Monay and Jaye drove into the church parking lot at the same time. When the girls walked into church, all eyes were on them. They were looking good. Jaye wore a black Armani suit with a wide black and white brim hat; Dasha had on a Larry Lavin black jumpsuit that camouflaged her stomach; and Monay wore a red Michael Kors suit that complemented her complexion. The ladies took their seats and spoke to some of the gentlemen who were checking them out.

~

Pinkeye stepped out of the house and looked down the street to see if Duce was coming. She saw a crowd of people standing around so she took off to see what was going on.

"Hey Pinkeye," someone called out from the crowd. "The paramedics just took Duce to the hospital."

"What happened?" Pinkeye asked.

"Little Bit saw Duce beating up her brother, so she jumped in and beat up Duce with a stick. It don't look good, Pinkeye."

Moments later the police were at Chicken's house looking for Little Bit. The officers brought Little Bit out of the house in handcuffs. Pinkeye gave Little Bit the evil eye—letting her know that she was going to get her for beating up Duce.

Pinkeye got someone to drive her to the hospital and when she arrived, she saw Chicken coming out of the emergency room.

"What happened Chicken?"

"I was walking down the street, on my way home, when I saw Duce. He asked me if he could holla at me. Duce accused me of lying—talking about I told you that he stole your money."

"Well how did Little Bit get in it?"

"Duce punched me in the face and when I hit the ground he started kicking me in the head. I felt like my head was going to explode."

Pinkeye saw the blood on the wrapped bandage around Chicken's head. "I was told that your sister beat Duce with a stick until he was unconscious. You know I am going to beat her up when I see her."

"You wrong Pinkeye," said Chicken. "What was my sister suppose to do—just stand there and let Duce kill me?"

"Fuck that," said Pinkeye, "her ass is mine."

Pinkeye stormed into the hospital and saw Duce's wife talking to a doctor. Pinkeye was furious. *What is her ass doing here?*

She walked over to the doctor, introduced herself, and told the doctor that Duce lived with her.

The doctor looked puzzled and said to Pinkeye, "Miss, this lady here told me that she is the patient's wife."

"Yes, she is his wife, but they are not together."

"But we are not divorced," said Duce's wife, "so that means you have no say-so in any matters when it comes to my husband."

Before Duce's wife could say another word, Pinkeye punched her in the face. The doctor ran to call security, but by the time security got there, Pinkeye had beat the shit out of Duce's wife and left the hospital.

When Pinkeye got home, she called the hospital and pretended like she was Duce's mother (his mother died ten years ago). The nurse told Pinkeye that Duce was doing fine and that he was staying overnight for observation. Pinkeye had mixed emotions. She was relieved that Duce was not seriously hurt, but she was angry with him for getting into trouble.

If Duce had only brought his ass straight to my house, he would not be in the hospital.

She went on with her dinner. With everything going on, she had forgot about Monay, Jaye, and Dasha coming over for Sunday dinner. She had less than an hour to finish cooking.

~

Duce woke up with a bad headache. But he didn't care about that; all he could think about was getting Little Bit and Chicken.

Duce was shocked when his wife walked into his hospital room.

"What the hell happened to you?" he asked.

"That stank bitch of yours hit me in the face because I told her that you are still my husband. I am going to take a warrant out on her."

"You are not going nowhere, but carry your ass home and clean up that nasty house. Coming in here, looking a mess with your hair standing on your head. Get out of here."

Duce's wife ran out of his room and swore that she would never go to him for anything—ever again.

Deep down inside, Duce knew he was wrong for beating Chicken. He picked up the phone to call Pinkeye. She answered on the first ring.

"Hey baby," said Duce.

"Duce, if you had come straight to my house, all this stuff would have never happened."

"Damn Pinkeye. Let me tell you what happened. All I was trying to do was holla at Chicken. But then, he started talking loud and talking slick out of his mouth. Then his crack head sister hit me in the head with a stick. She snuck up on me from behind."

"Oh is that right? When I see Little Bit—her ass is mine," said Pinkeye.

"I'm suppose to get out of the hospital tomorrow. Can you pick me up?"

"Yeah."

"See you tomorrow," Duce said and he hung up the phone not realizing how lucky he was to have Pinkeye by his side.

~

Jaye felt light as a feather after church service. "I needed that," she said. "The Holy Spirit was in God's house today!"

Dasha prayed and cried. She had a lot on her mind.

Jaye wanted to help but Dasha had not said anything about her pregnancy. So Jaye decided to wait until Dasha was ready to talk.

Jaye also noticed that Monay had a big smile on her face during the church service.

"Monay, you sure look happy," said Jaye.

"Yes, I am happy. I prayed that Maleake will ask me to marry him."

"Oh that's nice," said Jaye.

What Jaye really wanted to say was—"You fool! You need to pray that the Lord will take Maleake out of your life."

Monay wanted to hurry to Pinkeye's house and eat so that she could get home and set things up for Maleake. She thought about the look on Jaye's face when she told Jaye what she prayed for.

I am glad Jaye did not say anything negative. Because church or no church—I would have let her have it. I would have told her to stay out of my video and get her own with Jackson. Jaye don't know nothin' about being in love. I don't think she's ever been in love. Yes, Maleake might lie to me, but one thing for sure, he loves me.

Monay noticed that Dasha looked sad. "Did you hear what I said Dasha? Are you all right?"

"I'm fine," said Dasha. "Why you ask?"

"You look like you have a lot on your mind. Do you want to talk?"

"No, I'm okay."

"Girl, I am starving. I know Pinkeye threw down," said Monay. "Has Pinkeye said anything to you about what she wants to talk to us about?"

"No," said Dasha, "I guess she will tell us at dinner."

Monay parked in front of Pinkeye's house and Jaye parked behind her. Before Monay and Dasha could get out of the car, Chicken was in their face—pointing to his bandaged head.

"What happened to you, Chicken?" Monay asked.

"Hey Squeetie," said Chicken who was drunk as hell, "Duce beat me up for nothing."

Jaye walked up. "Did I hear you say that Duce beat you up?"

"Yeah," Chicken said. "Duce said that I told Pinkeye that he took the money that she made from her selling party. Then he punched me in the face and started kicking me. My sister busted Duce and knocked him unconscious. The police picked up my sister and took her to jail. I went to get her out but her bond cost too much."

"Well, are you going to press charges on Duce's ass for beating you?" Jaye asked.

"I don't know. You know how Pinkeye is," said Chicken.

"Forget Pinkeye," Jaye said, "maybe Duce will get some time in jail and Pinkeye will get over his no-nothing ass."

Pinkeye was looking out of the window and saw Chicken talking to the girls.

"Look at him talking. And look at Jaye getting all the information so that she can run her Ms. Social Worker role on me. Duce is my man and I don't care what Jaye or nobody else says. Chicken out there running his damn mouth. I know when I ask the girls to help me with my selling party, they are going to think the money is for Duce."

Pinkeye went to the door and yelled, "Y'all swamp coochies need to come in here and eat." Chicken walked away.

The smell of homemade rolls hit the girls in the face when they entered the house. Pinkeye had laid out her special dishes. Her table decor looked nice. She always knew how to hook up a dinner and her house was always as clean as a whistle.

"Pinkeye, where are your girls?" Jaye asked.

"They've gone to the movies."

Jaye tried to make small talk. Pinkeye went into the kitchen and Dasha followed her.

"Pinkeye, what do you want to talk to us about?" Dasha asked.

"I will talk to y'all after we have dinner. Dasha, what was Chicken talking about?"

"Chicken said that Duce beat him up because Duce thought that he (Chicken) told you that Duce took your money."

"Did you tell Jaye and Monay that I told you that Duce stole my money?" Pinkeye asked.

"No," said Dasha.

"What did Jaye say?" Pinkeye asked.

"What did Jaye say about what?" Jaye asked standing at the kitchen door.

"Nothing," said Pinkeye, "I was asking Dasha what did you say about helping her decorate her shop."

"Oh," said Jaye. She knew Pinkeye was lying but she did not push the issue.

Pinkeye had decided that she was not going to fool with Jaye about the incident between Chicken and Duce. Pinkeye needed help with her next party. *I'll let that bullshit that Jaye says go in one ear and out the motherfucking other. I would have had my money, but I paid a bill instead. But that's none of Jaye's business.*

They sat at the table, ate dinner, and reminisced about the good old times—growing up in the hood.

"Pinkeye, you out did yourself with this dinner," said Monay.

"Thanks," said Pinkeye.

"By the way," said Monay, "what do you want to talk to us about?"

Jaye looked up at Monay. She had no idea that Pinkeye wanted to talk to them about something.

"I was going to wait until we finished eating dinner but I guess I can ask now. I need help with this selling party that I am trying to have at the end of this month."

At first no one responded. Then, Dasha spoke up. "Pinkeye is trying to buy her girls back-to-school clothes."

"I thought you bought their clothes from your last party?" Jaye asked.

"I had something I had to do with that money," said Pinkeye.

"Chicken said something about Duce taking your money," said Jaye.

"I don't know who took my money. Duce brought that low budget bitch, Pea, in my house. I don't know what happened. I was asleep. Duce said that while he was in the bathroom, Pea went into my bedroom and took my money."

Jaye could not believe what Pinkeye said. *I know Pinkeye don't believe that bullshit. Pea is too scared to death of Pinkeye to take anything from her. Duce took that damn money and now she's trying to take up for his sorry ass.*

"I can help you," said Dasha. Monay also agreed, but Jaye rolled her eyes. Pinkeye got up from the table and went into the kitchen.

Jaye hollered. "How much you need?"

"I need about a thousand to have a party," said Pinkeye.

"A thousand," said Jaye, "we should all put together and buy your girls' school clothes. That would be less than a thousand. But no—like always you got to have a house full of people."

"Look Jaye," said Pinkeye, "I'm trying to make a profit."

"Why? So you can help Duce?" Jaye asked. "Chicken told us what happened and that he is going to press charges against Duce's black ass."

"Fuck Chicken," said Pinkeye. "So what's up? Are you going to help me out or what?"

Pinkeye knew that when it came to her daughters, Jaye would always be there.

"I hope you don't fuck around and give Duce's stank ass my money," Jaye said.

Pinkeye just looked at Jaye. Pinkeye always kept a hustle going on. Deep down within, she knew that she really needed to stop having selling parties and move out of the projects.

Jaye looked around Pinkeye's house. Even though Pinkeye had painted so many times over the years, you could see the nicotine on the walls from people smoking at her parties.

"Pinkeye, when will you need the money?" Jaye asked.

"By next week."

"Well I'll bring my part on Thursday," said Jaye.

"One more thing," said Pinkeye. "Could y'all help me cook the food and pick up things that I'll need?"

"Sure," said Monay and Dasha.

Jaye told Pinkeye that she would get back with her on that. "Girls I got to go and help Ma rearrange her furniture; and later, Jackson is coming over to my house. Pinkeye, the dinner was good," said Jaye.

"The food surely was good," Monay said. Dasha nodded.

"Well Pinkeye, I will talk to you before the week is out." Jaye left.

Chicken saw Jaye getting in her car. "Hey Squeetie," he said. "I talked to my sister and she told me that her court date is next week."

"What is she being charged for?"

Chicken told Jaye that the police officers told him that his sister was being held on attempted murder charges.

"WHAT! She tried to kill Duce?" Jaye asked.

"No, she was trying to protect me but Duce told the police that my sister tried to kill him. Squeetie, I think my sister is sick and I know that she can't survive being in prison."

"Chicken, you need to get a good lawyer to represent her. I will talk to you later."

Monay and Dasha left about five minutes after Jaye.

"Is that Pea standing over there flagging down cars? She better hope Pinkeye doesn't see her," said Monay. "Somebody told me that all three of Pea's children are in foster care. Did you know that?"

"Girl Maleake is coming over my house tonight and he said that he is going to spend the night. I did not want to say anything to Jaye about him because I know she would have talked against it. Why are you so quiet?" Monay asked. "You've been quiet all day."

"I'm okay," said Dasha. "I'm stuffed from eating so much."

"Well I guess next weekend, we will be at Pinkeye's house helping with her selling party. I was surprised that Jaye agreed to help out Pinkeye," said Monay.

"You know all Pinkeye has got to say is what her girls need and Jaye will be right there," said Dasha.

Monay pulled in front of Dasha's house. "I'll see you Friday at Pinkeye's."

"Okay," said Dasha.

Monay headed home with Maleake on her mind.

~

Mike is heated because he can't get in touch with Dasha.

"I know that bitch ain't trying to play me. I need to get in contact with my boy Dink and let him know that I'll be getting out of here soon. It's on when Dasha brings her ass up here. She better be talking right. I don't wanna hear nothing about being busy."

"Yo Mike, you gotta phone call," an inmate hollered.

Mike took the phone. "Hello."

"This Dink. What's up baby boy?"

"Nothing man. Just chillin."

"I heard you were getting out soon."

"Yeah man."

"Man niggurs be tripping. Money is live out here since you been locked up and I know you trying to get on board when you get out."

"Man what's up with Pop and Maleake?" Mike asked.

"No one told you–Pop got killed three years ago."

"WHAT!"

"Yeah man. He got tricked up by a niggur up in Huntersville—some young head."

"I have not heard from Maleake in three years," said Mike. "Yo Dink, have you seen Dasha?"

"Naw man. I don't see much of her but I know that she is remodeling her shop. Hey Mike, my time is up. I'll holla at you next week, same time."

~

As soon as Dasha turned the key to unlock the door, she heard the phone ring. "I know that's Mike calling. I'm not going to answer. I hope he got the money that I sent. I told him that I would visit him this weekend. I will send him a letter explaining that I have something important to do concerning my shop. I know he is going to be mad."

The phone rang again and she pretended that she did not hear it. She ran her bath water, undressed, and looked in the mirror. "I have gained at least 15 pounds. I know if I go see Mike, one look at me, and he will know that I'm pregnant. I would not want him to pull me close to him. And, if I pulled away, I know he would get mad."

Dasha got in the tub and relaxed. She felt her baby move. She thought about the ultra sound that she was scheduled to have at her next doctor's appointment.

"There is so much that I need to do before I have my baby. Monay mentioned a baby shower and I need to let her know what date I would like to have the shower."

Dasha got out of the tub feeling better. Her phone rang again.

"I wish I had a caller ID. It could be one of the girls calling to check on me, but I'm still not going to answer. I don't want to answer and it's Mike.

She got into bed, closed her eyes, and thought about the night that she conceived. The passion that overwhelmed her body filled her eyes with tears. "I've never felt that way before. But I know some things just can't be." Feeling lonely and helpless, Dasha dozed off to sleep.

~

Jackson tried calling Jaye on her cell phone. No answer—so he left a message. Since she wasn't home yet, he decided to take his time and take the long drive to Jaye's house.

Jackson drives a 2005-745 BMW—black-on-black. Heads turn when he drives down the street. Standing six feet and five inches tall, Jackson is good looking with smooth dark skin.

He worked hard over the years to get to where he is today. When he was 13 years old, he lost both of his parents in a car accident. His mother's sister raised Jackson like he was her own child. She sent him to private schools. He ranked number one in his high school graduating class and from there, he went on to earn his bachelors and masters degrees from Howard University. Jackson worked for six years before going into business for himself—opening a men's designer clothing store. He made a profit his first year. Later, he opened two more stores. Now, he owns four men's clothing stores.

Jackson wants to give Jaye so much. Even though Jaye talks about one day having her own business—a group home for boys—Jackson wants Jaye to have her own ladies' designer clothing store. He feels that Jaye could make good money with a designer store. She has excellent taste in clothes; she is a fine dresser; and on the selfish side, he loves to see her dressed in suits.

The sound of his cell phone interrupted his thoughts. "Hi baby. Are you on your way?" Jaye asked.

"Yes Boo, but I need to run by the ABC store to buy a bottle of wine."

"Okay," Jaye said, "I have to run back to Pinkeye's house. I forgot to get the rolls that she baked for my mom. I will call you when I'm on my way home."

As soon as Jaye parked, Pinkeye's girls saw her and ran to the car.

"Auntie Jaye," the girls said and gave Jaye a hug.

Jaye saw Chicken sitting on his front porch looking sad with his head hung. She told the girls that she would be right back and went over to see if Chicken was all right.

"Hey Chicken," she said. "Are you okay?"

When Chicken looked up at Jaye, she could tell that he had been crying.

"I'm okay," he said, "I was just thinking about my sister."

Jaye gave Chicken a business card of a lawyer who might be able to help Little Bit.

"Thanks Squeetie. I heard that Duce will be discharged from the hospital tomorrow."

"Don't worry yourself about Duce. You just contact that lawyer about getting help for Little Bit."

"I will call the lawyer tomorrow."

From her living room window, Pinkeye watched Jaye and Chicken talk. She moved away from the window when she saw Jaye walking toward the house. Jaye walked in and called out. Pinkeye came from the kitchen with the rolls in her hand.

"What was you and Chicken talking about?"

"Nothing really."

Pinkeye gave Jaye a look like she knew that she was lying. She handed Jaye the rolls.

"Thanks," said Jaye. "I will give you a call before the week is out and thanks again for Ma's rolls."

Pinkeye walked Jaye to the door. Chicken was still sitting on his porch.

I wonder what Jaye handed Chicken.

~

Jaye called Jackson back to let him know that she would be home in 20 minutes, but he did not answer. Jackson left his cell phone in his car when he stopped to talk to a lady who, waved to him as she was walking down the street. She looked familiar—like someone he dated in college.

"Forgive me for staring. I'm surprise to see you here in my hometown."

Right away she knew who Jackson was. "I work here now. Maybe we can get together sometimes?"

"Thanks, but no thanks," said Jackson. "I am dating someone."

"I see," she said. "Well here's my card and I will be waiting."

When Jackson got back into his car, he noticed that Jayed had called. He immediately called her back.

"Hi baby."

"Damn Jackson, why didn't you answer your phone?"

"I happened to run into an old friend and left my phone in my car."

"Someone I know?"

"Naw Baby. You don't know her."

"Her!"

Jackson could hear it in Jaye's voice that she was jealous—he liked that.

"Just get your ass around here. I am home now."

Jaye had things just right for Jackson. The lights dimmed—clean cotton Yankee candles burning that emitted a clean fresh scent—and a Will Downing CD playing softly. Jaye loved Will Downing. She thinks Jackson has a sexy voice like him. She thought about how much she enjoyed the way Jackson made love to her, but she does not want to be tied down to one man.

She opened her bedroom drapes. An orange hue from the sun going down gave the room a sweet warmness. As soon as Jaye heard Jackson pull in the driveway, she went in the bathroom and ran water in the tub with lots of bubble bath.

Moments later, she opened the door for Jackson. He walked in and admired the way Jaye had set the romance. Jackson followed Jaye in the bathroom and joined her in the tub.

The night has just begun. I love Jaye so much. I will give her anything.

Waiting on Time

Dasha relaxed on her sofa feeling stuffed after having a nice dinner at Pinkeye's house. She felt her baby moving. She closed her eyes and rubbed her stomach.

Dasha pondered over her plans as a single mom. She isn't worried about her finances—she knows that she can take care of her child. She has five months before her baby is born. Two months after that, Mike gets out of prison.

Crazy thoughts were going through Dasha's head about how Mike will react when he finds out about her baby. Maybe she would sell the shop and move to Northern Virginia—just to get away from him.

Two things she knew for sure—she would never put her child in danger and she was not going to visit Mike anymore. But, she would—at least for now continue—to send him whatever he needed.

"I must concentrate on having a healthy baby and not being stressed out."

After having a talk with the Lord, Dasha felt excited about being a mother. She thought about baby names and how she was going to decorate the nursery.

Thinking about her baby, she fell asleep. The phone interrupted her sweet dreams. She answered.

"Oh, you want to answer your phone now," Mike said. "Bitch I been calling you all day and I don't appreciate you hanging up on me. What kind of stuff you on?"

Without saying a word, Dasha hung up the phone. She had promised herself that she would not let Mike upset her anymore.

I have my baby to think about. I would love for Mike to be my baby's daddy, but he is not, so it is best for me to stay away from him.

Mike was furious with Dasha after she hung up on him. "I need to get in contact with my boy Dink to find out what's up. Dasha knows I don't play."

Mike's mind was racing. "What kinda stuff is she on? If I find out that Jaye is putting stuff in Dasha's head about ditching me, by any means, Jaye has got to go. Dasha is my ticket to getting back on my feet when I get out."

He looked in his book for Dink's phone number. He would call him Friday—that's when open phone time was allowed.

"Dasha better come up here this weekend and talk to me about what is going on. If I find out that she has another niggur, oh man, I can't wait to get the fuck up out of here!

Oh yes, here is Dink's number."

~

Duce called Pinkeye and told her to send a cab to pick him up from the hospital. She told him that she would call him back as soon as the corner was clear.

"I don't want niggurs standing on the corner when you come home. For sure, they would try and start something."

Pinkeye kept looking out the window. "Damn, don't niggurs ever go home?"

When everyone was gone, she called Duce.

"The corner is clear. I will call a cab now. You come to my house and not to that funky wife of yours. Do you hear me Duce?"

"Damn, I hear you Pinkeye."

A nurse handed Duce discharge papers to sign. She also gave him prescriptions to be filled.

"How I am going to get this medication without money or insurance?" The nurse did not answer him. "Well, I guess Pinkeye will have to pay for it."

Duce sat in a wheelchair in the lobby, while he waited for a cab. When the cab arrived, a nurse took Duce to the car and ten minutes later the cab pulled in front of Pinkeye's house. Pinkeye came out of the house wearing a short skirt and a white stomach shirt. She paid the cab driver, grabbed Duce by the arm, and twisted her ass back into the house.

From his living room window, Chicken watched Pinkeye and Duce. *If I had a gun, I would blow Duce away.*

~

Monay woke up to find Maleake and the five hundred dollars that she promised to give him—gone. He left a note telling her that he had to go and take care of some business for his mother and that he would call her later. She smiled.

"I knew my baby would not leave without letting me know something."

Monay kept replaying in her mind—Maleake making love to her last night; she hoped the same would happen again next weekend and every weekend throughout the holidays.

"Christmas is four months away. I need to start picking up extra shifts at work so that I can give Maleake a nice Christmas. I also need to talk to the girls to see what plans they have for Christmas and New Years."

~

Dasha felt good after a good night's sleep. While she cooked scrambled eggs and sausage, a song came on the radio that reminded her of Mike and the good times they use to have. *Looking back, it wasn't all good—when Mike disrespected me and even beat me.* Dasha quickly shook those thoughts out of her mind. She ate, got dressed, and went to work.

When Dasha arrived at her shop, a work crew was working on her building. Dasha got out of the car and started walking down the sidewalk to her shop. She noticed Mike's friend, Dink, standing across the street looking at her.

"Oh shit." When she turned around he was gone. "I wonder if he saw my stomach."

Dasha felt sick and dizzy. A worker noticed her and asked if she was okay. "I'm fine, thank you" said Dasha. She went into the shop, picked up the phone, and called Pinkeye to tell her about Dink.

"Hello."

"What took you so long to pick up the phone?" Dasha asked.

"Damn Dasha. I'm getting my freak on. Duce got out of the hospital today. What's up?"

"Nothing. I will call you later." Dasha was disappointed that she could not talk to Pinkeye about seeing Dink. She said a prayer and got herself together before her first customer arrived.

~

Jaye really sexed Jackson up last night. When she awakened, she saw the money that he had left. One thousand dollars was on her dresser and a note telling her how much he loved her.

Jaye was overwhelmed with the money. She called her office to let her secretary know that she would be coming in late. As soon as she finished talking to her secretary, her phone rang. It was Monay.

"What's up," said Monay.

"Well, well," said Jaye, "you sound happy this morning. Maleake must have put a hurting on you."

Monay giggled—sounding like a bride on her honeymoon. Jaye rolled her eyes to the ceiling thinking about Maleake's sorry ass taking advantage of Monay.

"So what have I done to get this early morning call from you?" Jaye asked.

"Oh, I'm calling to see if you have planned anything for the holidays. I hope we can all get together for the holidays. You know I like planning early."

"I know that's right."

"Well I was thinking," said Monay, "that we could rent a place for a New Years party and have Thanksgiving dinner at your house."

"That's cool with me."

"I will give Dasha and Pinkeye a call to see if they like the plans," Monay said.

"Okay," said Jaye, "let me know all the details at Pinkeye's party this Friday. Peace."

Jaye remembered that it was time for her annual medical check-up. She called and made an appointment for the following week.

After she showered and dressed, she called her mother.

"Hi Mom."

"Hi Baby Girl. How are you doing this morning? Did Jackson come over last night?"

"Yes, he did. That's why I am calling you. Mom, Jackson gave me a grand last night."

"You go girl. What are you planning to do with the money?"

"Well Mom, I know I can pay for two classes with the money."

"Jaye, you need to stick with Jackson."

"Mom, I will call you later."

"Why is it that when I say something about your relationship with Jackson, you brush me off? You better listen to your mother."

"Mom, I am not in love with Jackson."

"Okay, but you are going to miss your blessing Jaye."

"Mom, I've got to go. I will talk to you later."

Jaye looked in the mirror. She had on a Chanel black suit with a wide collar blouse and a pair of Michael Kors boots. She knew she looked good. Jaye thought about what Monay said about Christmas and New Years.

"I hate putting myself out there when it comes to Monay and that sorry man of hers. I know she's going to work a lot of overtime so she can give him a good Christmas. Christmas is coming. I know I've got to hook Jackson up with some real stuff."

~

Pinkeye tore Duce off "real decent in bed", as she would say. Duce told Pinkeye he wanted to live with her and nurse himself back to good health. He promised Pinkeye that he would get a job once he was back on his feet.

"Duce you know I want you here with me, but you keep running back to your swamp coochie wife."

"Pinkeye, I only go over there to see my children. That's all."

That was what Pinkeye wanted to hear. "I love you Duce and I will do anything to keep you," she said.

Things were coming together like Pinkeye planned. It was time for her to make money on the side. She wanted to quit her part-time job and have at least two selling parties a month. That way she would be home more, since Duce is now living with her. She didn't like leaving her girls around no man unless it was their father, and at this point she did not trust Duce alone with her girls.

Pinkeye took a shower and got dressed. She put on a short black halter dress with a lift bra, an ankle chain, and clipped on a long ponytail with blonde streaks.

Pinkeye wanted to shop early for her party; she decided to ask Monay, Dasha, and Jaye to give her the money today. When she called Monay and Dasha, they both said okay.

She hesitated about calling Jaye. "I sure hate to call Jaye, when I know she promised to give me the money on Thursday." She dialed Jaye's number.

"Hello Jaye, this is Pinkeye. I'm calling to see if I can get the money for the party today so that I can go shopping early."

"Yes," said Jaye, "and I will bring the money to you before I go to court."

Pinkeye was shocked. *Damn—for once the bitch did not talk shit.*

Putting the Rush On

Mike could not wait to talk to Dink on Friday.

"Stuff is happening too fast. My time to get out is getting closer and Dasha is acting crazy. I wonder what kind of stuff she's on. She knows I plan to live with her after I'm released.

The parole board told me that when I get out, I should live in a neighborhood that is crime and drug free. Dasha better have a good reason for pulling this. Dink said that she's been working on her shop. Maybe she is getting ready to make some real money. I better play my hand right."

Mike began to get paranoid. Things had changed—He had changed. He looked around his cell. He looked at the walls. It seemed like the walls were sucking him in. Mike knew that when he got out—no matter what—he would never go back.

I've been locked up for nine years—nine long years. And, I don't plan on coming back to prison. Dasha better act right. She is my ticket. But, she's beginning to mess with my head. She stopped coming to see me. I'm going to drop her a letter.

Mike will go berserk if he thinks he is being clowned. That is one of his psycho crazy patterns that he developed after being raised by a mother who constantly told him that he would never amount to anything, and a father who was a drunk. Mike swore that he would never let anyone clown him again, not even Dasha.

~

Jaye looked at her watch. "Damn, I have 30 minutes before court starts. Let me swing by Pinkeye's and give her this money."

She drove up in front of Pinkeye's unit—niggurs standing on the corner shooting dice. Chicken came out on the porch when he saw Jaye pull up.

"Hi Squeetie. Can I holla at you for a minute?"

"Chicken, I don't have that much time."

"I just want to let you know that Duce is over Pinkeye's house. I saw him when the cab brought him. He just got out of the hospital."

"Oh hell," said Jaye, "well I won't be long."

"Squeetie, my sister has a court date soon. They are talking about giving her five years for malicious wounding and I can't afford that lawyer you told me about."

"I will talk to you about that later, Chicken."

Jaye walked up to Pinkeye's front door. Before she could knock, Pinkeye opened the door. Jaye handed her the money and gave Pinkeye a serious look, but Pinkeye played it off. She knew that if she bucked, Jaye was going to go off.

"Thanks," said Pinkeye.

Jaye could see Duce's sorry ass stretched out on the sofa. Jaye was furious when she left and Pinkeye knew it.

"She's my girl, but I be damned if I will let Jaye talk stuff to me about Duce living in my house."

"One thing I can say though, Jaye has always made sure that my girls have all the latest fashions. She buys them nothing but the best—high price designer coats and shoes—things that I can't afford.

Monay and Dasha give my girls birthday and Christmas presents, but Jaye buys for them all the time. And, she has bought them more since they have been getting good grades. I really appreciate Jaye, but damn, she wants to run your life and shit."

Duce called Pinkeye and asked who was at the door. "It was Jaye, she dropped off something to me."

"I'm glad she didn't come in. I'm not feeling her right now with her nasty comments. It feels good to lay my head down after running the streets for six days before this bullshit happened to me. I don't give a damn what your bourge friends say, especially that high-class bitch Jaye."

~

Jackson was thinking about asking Jaye to marry him. He hoped that Jaye would say—yes. He had big plans for her. Jackson considered saying something to Jaye's mother about getting engaged, but he knew Jaye would get upset if she wasn't the first to know.

"If everything goes well, I will buy Jaye an engagement ring in New York. I know she is going to want a big wedding and that's what she will get. I am ready to settle down and Jaye is who I want to spend the rest of my life with."

Jackson always gives Jaye the best. He wants to give her the money to open up a group home. Jackson has never told Jaye how much money he makes. His clothing stores did well last year. His business grossed over six million dollars, and for three consecutive years, it was voted the number one men's clothing store by Fashional International.

"Jaye is the woman that I've been looking for since I finished college and started my own business. She would be a good mother for my children and with my high expectations and her smarts, we can't go wrong."

~

Dasha was determined to have a good day in spite of everything that was going on in her life. Her regular customers were pleased about the remodeling of her shop. She added a facial and nail salon, and a barbershop. She planned to hire three stylists and a barbershop manager. For a touch of class, Dasha will serve wine and cheese trays and have smooth jazz playing on a Bose sound system. She wants to attract working moms who are juggling a family, but still want to take time out to pamper themselves and look good.

Dasha had a lot on her mind. She thought about her child's future—and if something happened to her, who she would want to take care of her child.

Dasha lost her aunt about five years ago, and her aunt was all the family that she ever knew. She knew how important it was to have all legal documents in place before she had her baby. She wanted the peace of mind knowing that if something happened to her, that her child would be well taken care of. Jaye was the only person that she would want to raise her child. She was positive that her child would have a good life with Jaye.

A lady walked in the shop and asked Dasha if she was taking walk-ins. She looked familiar but Dasha could not remember where she had seen her. Dasha kept racking her brains trying to remember—and when she did—she wished she had not.

That's the woman I caught in my house with Mike. If that bitch thinks that I'm going to do her hair, she's crazier than I thought she was. She's got some nerve coming up here in my shop. She must don't know who I am. Then I guess not, because when we met, she was too busy with my man—in my bed—to remember me.

"Miss," said Dasha. I checked my appointment book. I have someone scheduled for the time that I gave you and I am booked up for the next three weeks."

Looking disappointed, she left the shop.

~

Jaye thought about Pinkeye walking around with short tight clothes on, trying to look sexy for Duce.

She will do anything to hold on to his sorry ass. Although Pinkeye looked neat, the clothes were too small and she is too big.

I was going to tell her that she didn't have to pay me back, but since I saw Duce—laid back like he's the man of her house—she'd better give me back every dime of my money. Now I got to help her with this ghetto selling party. I hate that I agreed to help Pinkeye this time. Instead of giving her the money, I should have bought her girls' school clothes—but knowing Pinkeye, she still would have her ghetto party.

I'm not going to stress about Pinkeye and Duce. Just as soon as that piece of shit gets back on his feet, he will be running back and forth to his crazy wife's house, beating people out of shit, getting his, and pushing his little drug packages. I'm surprise someone hasn't knocked off Duce. The more sorry he gets, the more Pinkeye loves his ass.

Pinkeye's day was going good. She bought lots of things for her party. Trying not to drop her shopping bags while she opened her screen door, she spotted Chicken walking down the street coming home from work. Any other time, Chicken would help Pinkeye with her bags, but this time he kept on walking and Pinkeye acted like she didn't see him.

When she opened her door, Pinkeye noticed a warrant hanging from the screen. It was for Duce.

Jaye persuaded Chicken to take out a warrant on Duce. That's what that paper was about that I saw her give to Chicken.

Pinkeye yelled, "Duce come here." He didn't answer.

She stomped down the hall to her bedroom. Duce was in a deep sleep. When she shook him, he sat straight up in the bed.

"Look at this, Chicken took a warrant out on you!"

"What," said Duce, "he must have thought that I told the police that Little Bit beat me with a stick. I was not going to tell the police. I was going to deal with that crack head myself. Oh! It's on now," said Duce. "I'm going to court and tell the judge that his sister tried to kill me when me and her brother were fighting."

"Well Duce, I don't have time for dumb stuff. It's money to be made."

"I'm with you on that," Duce said.

Pinkeye told Duce that she was going to quit her part-time job and stay home with him. For extra money, she decided to have selling parties twice a month.

"Damn Baby, I was thinking the same thing," Duce said.

He figured it would take him about four months to get himself together. He knew that he would be well taken care—now that Pinkeye would be home with him.

"Pinkeye's party is this weekend. Maybe I can get me a crap game going on in the back room."

Duce made his living on gambling and selling drugs—he never kept a job more than a week. Pinkeye knows all about Duce's life, but it does not matter to her.

Pinkeye started marinating her meats and moving furniture around to make room for the anticipated party crowd.

"I wish I could help you baby," said Duce, "but my body is too stiff."

"Duce I got this. Dasha and Monay are coming over to help me."

~

Jaye called Jackson on his cell.

"Hey Jaye, baby."

"Jackson, I really want to thank you for the money. You are so sweet.

By the way, my mother's birthday is the Sunday after we get back from New York. Will you come to her birthday dinner?"

"Sounds like a plan to me," said Jackson. "Do you need my help?"

"No, I already took care of everything. I really want things nice for her 60th birthday."

"Let's buy her a birthday present while we are in New York," said Jackson. "Oh by the way, I made our hotel and flight reservations."

"That sounds nice," Jaye said. "I will see you Saturday, at the airport."

Jaye wished that Pinkeye's party was on Saturday instead of Friday. Then she would have an excuse for not going to the party—she would be in New York.

Her phone rang. She thought it was Jackson so she did not look at her caller ID.

"Hey sexy, long time no see."

"Who is this?" Jaye asked.

"Oh, you forgot who I am?"

"Do me a favor," said Jaye.

"And what's that?"

"Lose my number," said Jaye and she hung up.

That nickel and dime old player calling me. It's time for me to fire a lot of my players and get focused. They cannot carry me where I'm trying to go.

Jaye called the university for registration information. After she took care of school business, she called the Department of Youth Services to obtain a package for opening a group home.

She had a lot of work ahead of her but she was determined to reach her goals—open up a boys group home, and get her Masters degree.

~

Dasha was tired when she got home. In addition to ten regular customers, she took in three walk-ins.

She ran her bath water, laid out a nightgown, and ate a snack. Then she got in the tub and relaxed.

She thought about her plans for how she was going to take care of her baby. She projected that her profit from her salon would increase more than fifty percent in one year. So far, she had spent ten grand on remodeling, and she hoped to make three times that amount a month after she hired additional staff. She also planned to buy a condo for a tax write-off.

After getting out of the tub, she checked her answering machine and ate some more. Mike had called and tried to leave a message, but the operator cut him off.

"I'm glad I missed his call. I know Mike was calling about money. I need my money for my baby. He is going to go off when I stop sending him money, but at this point I don't care. I need to think of my child first.

I know Mike is not going to except me being pregnant by another man. After Pinkeye's party this week, I will be taking on a new lease on life. I go for an ultra sound on next Monday. Jaye is so excited about giving me a baby shower. I am happy with my plans."

Dasha felt her eyes getting heavy. She turned off her lamp and went to sleep.

~

Monay stayed up late making plans for their New Years party and making a list for Christmas gifts. What she planned to buy Maleake was at the top of her list. After she tallied everything, she estimated that she would spend about twelve hundred dollars on just Maleake's gifts.

Monay was thinking about giving Maleake a key to her condo and asking him to move in with her. She wanted Maleake with her for the holidays. She dialed his cell phone number and let the phone ring six times before hanging up. *My baby must be fast asleep.*

She finished making her plans and decided to have Christmas dinner at her house since they were having Thanksgiving dinner at Jaye's. *The holidays are the only time that Jaye doesn't talk shit about Maleake, Mike, and Duce. It's a festive time. Everyone brings his or hers own cheer. Pinkeye always brings the most.*

Monay thought about last year's New Years party at Jaye's house. "No one made it home. It was just us girls because Jaye refused to have our men in her house.

Dasha can't get tossed with us this year because of the baby. Speaking of the baby, when will Dasha say something about her baby's father? I'm surprised Jaye has not said anything. I guess everyone is staying out of it."

Monay yawned and closed her eyes. She imagined watching Maleake, on Christmas morning, open all the beautifully wrapped gifts from her. She drifted off to sleep.

~

Pinkeye went shopping the next day for more stuff for her party. She went to the grocery store and bought shrimp, party wings, crab meat to make crab cakes, and party trimmings. She also went to the liquor store and bought six fifths of different liquor and eight cases of beer.

When she was leaving the ABC store, she saw Pea walking down the street. "Of all days—but I'll see that stank bitch again and then, I am going to beat the breaks off her stealing ass."

Pinkeye went to the mall. She ran into a couple of people from the projects and invited them to her party. She bought herself a black Echo jumpsuit and a pair of Echo shoes. "I know Jaye is going to be looking at me. She thinks everything that I wear is too tight. This is my ass and I can put whatever I want to put on it."

Pinkeye also bought clothes for Duce. She got him two pairs of jeans, two baseball caps, three shirts, and a pair of Air Force Ones.

"I am not going to have my man looking like shit. The only clothes that he has are the ones on his back. His dumb ass wife will not let him get his clothes. The reason why she is doing this is because her husband is living with me. If he weren't hurt, he would beat her ass and take his clothes.

Duce never mentioned anything about the hospital incident between his wife and me. I wonder if she took a warrant out on me. I need to ask Duce about that when I get back home."

Pinkeye looked at her watch—"Damn, I need to pick up Dasha at her beauty shop. I am glad that she let me use her car. Maybe I will have time to get my nails done at her shop."

There's Money to be Made

Word spread in the projects about Duce's crap game at Pinkeye's house. Maleake planned to go.

I hope Duce cleared that with Pinkeye because she does not allow no dumb shit around her daughters and Duce knows that. I know Monay and her crew will be there. No matter where Pinkeye lives and what she does, those girls are always there. I wonder sometimes if they are having sex with each other. Let me call this worrisome bitch. I know she's going to ask me about the five hundred dollars that she gave me and if everything worked out.

"Hey Monay."

"Hey baby. Did everything work out for you?"

"Yea, I took care of my business," he said with a smirk.

"Maleake, I need to talk to you."

"We can talk tonight, Monay. I'm going to Pinkeye's party. I need you to pick me up from my boy Snake's house."

"No problem," said Monay, "I will pick you up at 10:00."

Maleake started thinking about ways that he could get more money out of Monay.

"I know her ass is going to be all over me at the party. I'll act like I'm enjoying her shit. I need her money so I can get me another package. I will let Duce twirl it. He better not mess up my stuff."

Maleake spent six months in jail for selling drugs and he is still on probation. He has always had women take care of him and he has never had his own place. Monay thinks that Maleake lives with his sister and sometimes with his mother. But he really lives with Tara, one of his women who is getting tired of his lazy ass. She no longer wants to take care of him. She stopped buying food for the house and she stopped giving Maleake money.

Monay was glad to hear that Maleake was going to be at Pinkeye's party. She couldn't wait to talk to Maleake about moving in with her. But, what Monay did not know was that Maleake wanted to move in with her. Since his set-up at Tara's had changed, he was ready to leave Tara and move in with Monay.

"That bitch, Tara, is tripping. I need to find a way to move in with Monay. She lives better than Tara any day. Monay makes good money but the bitch is too needy.

When I move in with Monay, I will tell her that I work at night on a part-time job. That way I can spend the night with my other bitches and sell during the day while she is at work. I will break her off a little something from the money I make from selling a package. That way, it will look like I'm working and helping her out financially.

I know Monay won't put a price on me staying there. She'll be happy just cause' I moved in with her. Forget Tara. I am moving from one wised-up bitch to a dumber one. I like it when my plan comes together. And I be damned, if I will let that bourge-ass Jaye ruin this.

If Jaye starts running her mouth about me to Monay, I'll hit Monay in the head with, 'I was going to ask you to marry me baby' and then threaten to leave her. I know when I tell the dumb bitch that—she will do anything to keep me; and Jaye's ass will be out the back door.

Jaye won't fuck this up. I don't have time for bullshit! I got to get back on my feet. I'm ready to live like a king and I know Monay is going to make sure of that."

~

Mike is glad to see Friday come. He could make a call and his name was first on the list to use the phone. He planned to call Dink. Phone time was not until 1:00 p.m.; he had about two hours to wait.

Mike thought about the things he wanted Dink to check out for him. He needed a plan-B, just in case Dasha changed her mind about him living her. Mike's sister recently moved into a nice neighborhood, so he thought she would be his backup plan. If he didn't have a residing address to give the parole board before he was released, Mike would be sent to a halfway house until he was off probation.

He used his calling card so that he could call straight through.

"Hello."

"This Mike, Yo."

"What's up baby boy," said Dink. "Check this out. I saw your girl walking in her shop. Man she looks good. She put on weight and her hair has gotten long."

"Dink man, I need for you to keep an eye on her. Man she's been tripping. I have not seen her in a month and she has not sent me any money in two weeks."

"WORD!" Dink said. "I can do that for you."

"You said she put on weight?"

"True that," said Dink.

"The last time she was here her breast looked big."

"Maybe I will see your girl at Pinkeye's card party tonight. Duce plans to have a crap game going on in Pinkeye's back room. By the way, I told Maleake that you would be out soon."

"Damn Dink. I wish I was home. Does Pinkeye know that Duce is having a crap game in her house?"

"I don't know man."

"Has Pinkeye changed?"

"Naw man. She's still wilding out and busting niggurs in their shit. Duce is going to mess around and make Pinkeye fuck him up if he don't check with her first about that crap game. He knows Pinkeye don't play that around her daughters."

"Dink, my time is up. I will holla at you this time next week."

~

Pinkeye completed everything that she had to do for her party. She was glad that she was able to use Dasha's car to do her shopping. Pinkeye was excited about the money that she was going to make. She went into the bedroom to talk to Duce.

"What's up baby," he said.

"Duce, I just thought of something when I was out shopping. Do you know if that crazy ass wife of yours took out a warrant on me for beating her ass?

"Naw, I told her she'd better not do a damn thing."

Duce felt that the timing was just right to ask Pinkeye if he could make her some extra money by having a crap game during her party. He thought that if he said that she would make money, she would say yes. When he asked her, Pinkeye gave Duce a dirty look. But then she thought about the money and told him that it was okay.

"I'll see if Jaye will let my girls stay at her house."

Pinkeye never has her girls around gambling and weed smoking.

Pinkeye called Jaye. "Hey Jaye, this is me. I was calling to see if my girls can stay over your house tonight?"

"Sure. What time do you want me to pick them up?"

"Whenever you want to. Thanks Jaye. I will see you later."

Duce was smiling his ass off. His plan worked and he was not going to give Pinkeye a damn penny of the money from the crap game.

"I'm glad Pinkeye asked me if her girls could spend the night. Now I have a reason to leave early. Besides, those babies don't need to be around that kind of stuff. I know Duce is going to be selling weed. I left that lifestyle seven years ago and I'm not trying to get caught up in it again.

I be damned if I invite Jackson to that ghetto shit. He would go if I asked him to, but this is not his kind of party. Jackson has too much going on.

Oh shit! It's getting late and I need to pick up Pinkeye's girls, so that I can bring them to my house and then go back to Pinkeye's bullshitting party."

Twenty minutes after Pinkeye called, Jaye pulled up to pick up the girls. They were standing on the front porch with their overnight bags. As soon as they spotted Jaye, the girls ran and got in the car. Before Jaye could pull off, Chicken came over.

"Let me holla at you Squeetie."

Jaye got out of the car so the girls would not hear what Chicken was saying.

"Duce is planning on having a crap game in one of Pinkeye's back rooms and that's why she is sending her girls with you."

"Thanks for the info Chicken. I am only going to stay for a short time, then I am out," said Jaye. "I know you're not going to the party, Chicken."

"Hell no. She will not make money off of me tonight. I'll stay home and get drunk. Pinkeye thinks Duce wants her ass. But as soon as he gets back on his feet, he will be like a ghost. Duce is a grease motherfucker; one day he will get his," said Chicken.

~

Pinkeye had everything in place. The table was full of food. She was selling dinners and sandwiches. Her dinners were set at one price and she offered a free drink with every sandwich.

She estimated her profit to be two grand plus a cut off the top from Duce's crap game.

Pinkeye walked around, twisting back and forth. She knew she looked good. Her hair was in an up-do, with blonde and brown mixed hair hanging down in the front. She called Dasha to see if she was on her way with the ice.

"Hi Dasha, are you with Mo?"

"No, she is riding with Maleake."

"Do you have the ice?"

"I bought four bags. I'm almost at your house. Come out and get the bags."

She went out on the porch to wait for Dasha. Pinkeye saw Chicken on his porch drinking a beer. Dasha drove up and Pinkeye went to the car to get the ice. Chicken turned his back when he saw Pinkeye.

"It's cool Chicken," said Pinkeye, "you can come to the party if you want to."

"I'm okay," Chicken said.

Pinkeye filled the coolers with wine and ice. She had plenty of liquor and weed. The party was on.

"Dasha, you are looking cute tonight. You don't look like you are having a baby," Pinkeye said.

Dasha was glad to hear Pinkeye say that she looked good; but, she worried that Maleake and Duce would notice that she was pregnant.

"I know Pinkeye and Monay have not told them, but that's all I need—Duce and Maleake to know that I am pregnant. I'm only going to stay for a little while. I am glad that I drove so that I can leave when I want to."

Monay and Maleake walked in, and Dink followed. Dasha felt uneasy being in the same room with Dink and Maleake—both were Mike's running partners.

"Hi Ms. Dasha," said Maleake, "I see that you are remodeling your shop."

"Yes, I'm making some changes."

"I know it's costing you a pretty penny."

Dasha did not answer him.

Jaye walked in and Dasha was so glad to see her.

"Oh thank heaven! Jaye, I am so glad you are here. Now I know Dink and Maleake will be carrying their ass into another room, cause' they don't like you, Jaye."

Dasha and Jaye laughed as they watched Maleake and Dink walk down the hall to the back room.

Dasha felt relieved. She went in the kitchen and sat with Pinkeye. Monay and Jaye stayed in the living room. The party began to get crowded. Pinkeye took coats and directed people to what was what. All Pinkeye had on her mind was making money.

Dasha saw people whom she had not seen in a long time. She laughed at how awful they looked.

Jaye noticed that all the men were going to the back room.

"That stank ass Duce is back there gambling and making money off the top, and I know he is not going to give Pinkeye shit. I know I am not going to stay long with all of the wild shit that is about to jump off in here. Pinkeye needs to change her way of thinking. These motherfuckers in here don't give a shit about her. When this bullshitting party is over, Pinkeye won't have to worry about me coming to another one of her ghetto parties."

Then Jaye noticed Dasha talking to herself and looking like she had a lot on her mind.

"She needs to holler at a therapist for real-real. Since she's been pregnant, she's been staying home a lot.

And look at Monay over there. Her ass could eat a chunk of Maleake's sorry ass. She has been smiling the whole time we've been here. I know she's going to have his black ass spend the night with her and she won't get nothing out of it but a wet ass."

Jaye was bored. "It's 11:30. I am going to leave at midnight."

She went into the kitchen and sat with Dasha.

"What's up girl," said Jaye.

"Nothing. I feel a little tired. Smelling that weed is making me sick."

"Dasha you need to get out of here. All this smoke is not good for your baby."

That's all Dasha needed to hear. She went to tell Pinkeye that she was leaving.

Dink came from the back room. "Yo, aren't you Mike's old lady?"

"Yes," said Dasha and kept walking. Dasha could feel Dink watching her. Pinkeye saw the look on Dasha's face.

"Are you okay?" Pinkeye asked.

"I'm tired," said Dasha, "so I'm going to leave."

"Call me when you get home," said Pinkeye.

Jaye walked Dasha to her car and gave her a hug.

"Dasha," said Jaye, "you look like you have a lot on your mind. Is there anything you want to talk about?"

"Naw, just tired. It's been a long day."

"Call me when you get home," Jaye said.

Jaye walked back into Pinkeye's house. The smell of weed hit her in the face. She decided that staying at the party wasn't worth risking her job. "I have a profession to uphold." She went to find Pinkeye.

"Pinkeye I am leaving now. I need to pack for my trip. I will bring your girls home in the morning."

"Okay," said Pinkeye.

She knew Jaye was not going to stay long because this kind of party was not her cup of tea. "Fuck that. I am glad she is leaving. Now I can make this money without having Miss Social Worker checking everything out."

Jaye was glad to leave the party. Chicken saw her getting in her car.

"Hey Squeetie. Can I get your cell number in case I need you to help me with any paper work for my sister?"

"Sure," Jaye said and she gave Chicken her number.

Jaye's mind went back to Pinkeye's party. Something did not feel right to her. Pinkeye never had people in her house smoking weed and gambling. She knew that if she had said something to Pinkeye about that, she would have gone off.

"Her ass is going to learn the hard way. Duce staying with her—that is going to be her down fall."

On her way home, Jaye began thinking about Jackson. She was beginning to feel him. She thought about all the money that he gave her and about their trip to New York City.

Her phone rang.

"Hello," said Jaye.

"Why didn't you and Dasha tell me that you were leaving the party?" Monay asked.

"Monay, you were in the back room and I was not going back there."

"Why, because Maleake was back there?"

"Fuck Maleake. I did not want to be in that atmosphere," Jaye said. "I will talk to you before I leave tomorrow."

"Don't bother."

"What's that supposed to mean? You know what Monay, you are talking real crazy about now, and I don't have time for dumb shit."

"Oh you calling me dumb?"

"What the fuck. You need to stop drinking and get yourself together," said Jaye.

"I am together. I only had two drinks. You just don't like Maleake."

"No I don't like his ass and you should not like his ass either."

"Damn you Jaye," Monay said and hung up.

"That crazy bitch hung up on me," said Jaye. "Maleake's sorry ass has got her going. Now I know I need to get away from all of this. I'm glad Jackson and I are going to New York."

~

Dasha was glad to get home.

"Pinkeye never had a party like that before. I need to stay home and concentrate on building up my business. The remodeling will be finished next month and I must say—it's looking good."

Dasha put in hardwood floors. The craftsmanship around the shampoo bowls is brass. There is a pedicure and nail salon with black massage tables on one side of her shop. Throughout the shop is a Bose surround sound system and also long mirrors with a tint of gray. She is thinking about putting in a day care on the other side of the shop so that when she is working—her baby will be near her.

Dasha decided to buy a condo in downtown Norfolk. The development was down the street from a police department.

"I should not have to worry about Mike bothering me and my child. We should be safe living close to a police station. Even though I still love Mike, I know that he will never accept my child. So we can't ever be together."

Dasha thought about when Dink asked her if she was Mike's old lady. She wondered if Dink saw her stomach. She knew that Mike would find out when he got out of prison. Dasha quickly stopped thinking about Mike.

"When I get my new condo, I'll have a lot of packing to do for the move. I know my girls are going to help me."

She showered, ate a little, and then dozed off to sleep. She jumped when she heard her cell phone ring.

"Hello."

"I told you to call me when you got home."

"Oh Jaye. I forgot to call."

"Are you going to bed now?" Jaye asked.

"I can talk. What's up?"

"Girl can you believe Pinkeye had all that shit going on in her house. I am glad her girls are here with me. I'm glad that she still has respect for them."

"What time are you leaving tomorrow?" Dasha asked.

"Our plane leaves about 10:00 in the morning. I need to call Jackson to make sure. Dasha, I will talk to you tomorrow."

Jaye called Jackson.

"Hello."

"Baby this is Jaye. I was just calling to find out what time we are leaving tomorrow."

"Jaye, what are you doing up so late?"

"I went to Pinkeye's party."

"Oh, that's right," said Jackson, "and did you have a good time?"

"I will tell you about it on the plane."

"Okay. Jaye, our plane leaves at 10:30. I'll see you in the morning. Love you."

No More Time Wasted

Pinkeye had fifteen hundred stuffed in her bra and she still had time to make more money. She was closing her party down in two hours.

"Pinkeye, somebody is at the door," said Monay.

"Oh no—it's RaRa," said Pinkeye. "Bitch what you doing here? Somebody told me that you were locked up."

"Somebody told you a damn lie," said RaRa.

"Bitch you still making money?" Pinkeye asked.

"You damn right. They say it's hard out here for a pimp. Hell, it's hard out here for a whore."

"You still crazy as hell," said Pinkeye.

"Where your bourge-ass friends?" RaRa asked.

"Now you wrong. Can't nobody talk about them but me."

"I heard that," said RaRa. "Y'all still carry it like that."

"And you know that," said Pinkeye.

Monay looked at RaRa and rolled her eyes.

Pinkeye didn't notice Monay. Even though she was feeling good, Pinkeye stayed focused on making money.

She went in the back room to check on the card party. When she opened the door, Pea was standing by the window. She could not believe that Pea was in her house. Pinkeye lunged and knocked Pea so hard that Pea fell on Duce. He hollered when Pea fell on his leg.

"What the hell you doing letting that bitch in my house after she stole my money?" Pinkeye shouted at Duce.

She kicked Pea in the stomach. Pea lost her breath for a short time. Pinkeye pulled a switchblade from her bra and slashed Pea's face. Duce tried to stop Pinkeye but he was too slow getting up. Maleake grabbed Pinkeye. Monay heard the commotion and ran into the back room.

"Pinkeye stop!" Monay hollered.

But Pinkeye kept on beating Pea until she threw her out the front door. Pea fell on the ground and could not move. Pinkeye was heated. She went back into the house and cursed Duce out.

"Why did you let her in my house?"

"I thought you let her in." Duce said.

"Why would I let her in Duce?"

Since Duce had told Pinkeye that Pea took her money, he tried to play it off—like he had nothing to do with Pea being at the party.

"I was wondering why you let her in—especially since she stole your money. Damn baby, you beat the brakes off her ass."

Pea lay in Pinkeye's front yard holding her face. When Chicken saw Pea hurt, he called the ambulance.

Twenty minutes later the police and ambulance arrived. The officer asked Chicken what happened. Chicken told the police that he didn't know how Pea got hurt, and that she must have been at one of the other row houses.

Chicken knew that he could have gotten back at Duce by telling the police about the weed and gambling going on at Pinkeye's house. But Chicken said nothing about it to the police.

Monay looked out the window and saw the police. She went and got Pinkeye. "I hope Chicken isn't running his mouth, talking ass niggur," said Pinkeye.

When she saw the police walking over to her house she told Monay to turn down the music.

When the officer came up, Pinkeye acted like she did not know what was going on.

"May I help you officer?"

"Do you know Pea?"

"Yes, I know her."

"Do you know what happened to her?"

"No officer. When I saw your car lights, I came to my door to see what had happened."

After the officer left, Pinkeye went in the house and closed down the party.

An ambulance took Pea to the hospital.

Monay and Maleake left the party. She could not wait to get home so that she could sex-up Maleake. She put her hand on his private part while she was driving. He tried to act like he was falling asleep. "Not tonight. I will hit you in the morning." Monay was a little disappointed, but just having Maleake in bed with her—was good enough.

Monay was upset because Jaye and Dasha did not tell her that they were leaving. *Jaye was just mad because her man was not at the party. She probably got Dasha to leave.*

She pulled in her driveway. Maleake was so high that she had to help him out of the car and into the house. When she opened the front door, Maleake called her another woman's name. Mad as hell, she dropped him on the sofa.

Worn out, Monay took a shower and went to bed. She forgot Maleake was sleeping in the living room. The sound of him talking in his sleep woke her up. A few minutes later Maleake came in the bedroom, took off his clothes, and got in bed. Monay slid over to the edge of the bed. For the first time, she did not want Maleake to touch her.

She had a hard time falling asleep. All kinds of things were running through her mind—*Why would Maleake call me another woman's name? Maybe I'm moving too fast. Maybe I should not give him a key and ask him to live with me. Who is Linda?*

The delicious smell of eggs, bacon, and pancakes woke up Monay. She opened her eyes and saw Maleake standing beside the bed—holding a serving tray with fresh cut flowers. He served her breakfast in bed. Monay smiled and praised Maleake for cooking her breakfast.

That's all Maleake wanted to hear. Now he knew that Monay would let him move in.

Maleake started shooting game and before he could say another word, Monay said, "Maleake, I want you to move in with me."

"What did you say baby?"

"I said would you like to move in with me?"

Maleake did not want to seem anxious, so he decided not to give her an answer right then. "Let me think about it for a few days." He was pleased with his plan.

Monay was happy knowing that she and Maleake would spend the holidays together. She forgot all about asking him who Linda was.

"I know Maleake does not have a job, but I will take care of him until he finds one. Maybe I can help him get a job at the hospital. It would be like we are married. I know Jaye is going to have something to say. She needs to stop thinking about me and focus on Jackson."

~

Jaye was tired after only getting three hours of sleep. She showered and felt refreshed. Then she woke up Pinkeye's girls. They all got dressed and ate breakfast. Jaye put her suitcase in her car, packed the girls in, and took them home.

When she arrived to Pinkeye's house, they got out the car and saw blood stains on the porch. Pinkeye came to the door before the girls knocked.

"Ma, why is blood on the porch?" Pinkeye's girls asked.

Pinkeye lied and said, "One of Duce's friends cut his hand when he opened a bottle."

Jaye heard Pinkeye and asked, "Who cut their hand?"

"Oh, one of Duce's friends," Pinkeye said.

"Well, I will give you a call when I get back," said Jaye.

The girls gave Auntie Jaye a hug. Pinkeye thanked Jaye for letting the girls spend the night.

Jaye was on her way to the airport to meet Jackson.

Her cell phone rang.

"Hello."

"Hi Jaye. Are you at the airport?"

"Hi Mom. I am on my way to the airport."

"I thought Jackson was picking you up."

"Pinkeye had a party last night and her girls stayed with me; so I had to take them home this morning."

"Did you go to the party?"

"I went for a little while. Mom, Pinkeye never had a party like that before."

"What do you mean?"

"I will tell you about it when I get back. Jackson is waiting for me at curbside check-in. I'm just arriving at the airport. I'm about 10 minutes late."

"You have a safe trip. I love you Jaye."

"I love you too, Mom."

~

Pinkeye hugged her girls and told them that she was going to take them shopping for school clothes. The girls were so excited—they each wrote a shopping list.

Pinkeye made three grand from the party. She felt real good! She had enough money to buy her girls' school clothes and pay back Jaye, Dasha, and Monay. And after doing all of that—she would still have money to pay a few bills.

Pinkeye especially wanted to payback Jaye. "I know Jaye is going to have something to say about Duce— but at least I won't owe her a damn thing. She don't like the idea of Duce living with me, but that won't stop her from helping me with my girls.

Jaye will always make sure that my girls have school clothes and anything else that they need. She's always been good to my girls."

Pinkeye thought about the money that Duce made from his crap game. She went into the bedroom and saw Duce's money on the bedside table. "I hope he buys Christmas presents for his kids. I know he is not going to save a dime. If I can make fifteen hundred dollars a month from parties, I will be straight. I will tell Duce that he can't have any more crap games at my house."

All of a sudden, Pinkeye felt a sharp pain in her arm. "Damn! I think I hurt my arm when I hit Pea. The nerve of that bitch coming in my house after she stole my money. I did not give her a chance to say a word, I just hit her in her shit."

Pinkeye looked out her bedroom window and saw Chicken walking to the mailbox. "I wonder what Chicken told the police. I am not going to sweat that bullshit."

~

Jaye parked her car, grabbed her suitcase, and hurried to meet Jackson. He smiled when he saw her rushing to meet him.

Jaye could not ignore how different she felt when she saw Jackson. *Could I be having feelings for him?*

Jackson put his arms around Jaye's waist, pulled her close, and french kissed her. Then he whispered in her ear, "I have something for you when we get on the plane."

The kiss—the whisper—took Jaye by surprise.

They checked their bags and went to the boarding area. When they got on the plane, Jaye was surprised that Jackson had purchased first class tickets.

Oh, that was it. When Jackson said that he had something for me when we got on the plane, he was talking about sitting in first class.

Once the plane took off, Jackson took a credit card out of his wallet and gave it to Jaye. He told her that the credit card limit was whatever she made it.

Jaye could not believe it. *Jackson just gave me a credit card with no limit!*

Jackson laughed when he saw the look on Jaye's face. As she held the credit card tightly in her hand, Jaye felt her attraction getting stronger for Jackson.

"You know I love you Jaye."

Before Jaye realized it, she told Jackson that she loved him.

Jackson began kissing Jaye all over her face. A lady, who was sitting in a seat across from them, stared—with a jealous look—at the happy couple. Jaye noticed her and gave her more to look at. She kissed Jackson from his forehead down to his neck. The nosy passenger turned her head.

When the pilot announced that the plane would land in fifteen minutes, Jaye could not believe how fast they got there. She was use to the eight-hour drive that she often made to New York City.

Jaye could not wait to get to the hotel. She had plans for Jackson—like wearing the sexy teddy and pair of low cut thongs that she packed. She slipped the credit card into her Gucci wallet.

I know that I got to get rid of my other players. Those coupon niggurs can't touch Jackson. If I change my cell number, Jackson will think something is up. I will tell my players that I am going back to school and that I will not have time to see them because I have to study.

After they landed and got their bags, Jackson got a limo to take them to the hotel. Once they were checked in, Jaye rested while Jackson made reservations for dinner and a limo. He had three hours before his business meeting. Jaye walked passed him with a pair of black thongs on. His first look at Jaye—he felt his nature rising. He pulled Jaye close to him and kissed her all over.

"Not now," said Jaye, "I have a surprise for you when we get back from dinner."

~

Dasha felt good after a good night's sleep. Her first appointment was not until 11:00. She picked up the phone to call Pinkeye.

"Hello."

"Hi, Pinkeye."

"Why didn't you call me when you got home last night?"

"I knew you were busy with your party. Besides, Jaye called to check on me."

"I know Jaye got you to leave the party early."

"No she did not. The weed smoke was making me sick."

"What did Jaye say about the party?"

"Nothing, she was talking about her trip to New York."

"I am glad Jaye was not at the party when RaRa came," said Pinkeye.

"I know that's right."

"Even when we were in middle school, Jaye didn't like RaRa. And after I got in trouble hanging out with RaRa and ended up in jail, she never—ever—wanted me to be around RaRa. Hold on Dasha, I got another call.

Hello."

"This is May, I am calling to let you know that Harold died last night."

"Oh no! Thanks for calling May."

Pinkeye beeped Dasha back and told her about Harold.

"Are you all right?"

"I'm fine, I will talk to you later."

Duce heard Pinkeye crying. "What's up?" Duce asked.

"May just called and told me that Harold died."

"Now your ass in here crying over an old ass player."

"Fuck you Duce. Harold was my friend and he was good to my children."

"So what. The niggur died. He's just another dead old motherfucker. You act like you was in love with his ass. You need to let me punch you in your face. It's been two weeks." *That was Duce's way of saying that she hadn't given him some.*

Pinkeye decided not to pay attention to what Duce was saying. She went outside and told her daughters about Harold.

~

Dasha got dressed and headed to the shop. She thought about how sad Pinkeye sounded on the phone when she was talking about Harold. He was Pinkeye's player for ten years—way before Duce came into the picture.

When Dasha arrived at her shop, she noticed an envelope stuck in the door. It was a letter from Mike. She wondered why he did not send the letter to her house. Then she remembered that Mike never had her home address. Just seeing his name on the letter made her nervous.

"I can't read this now. I will wait until I get home. He is not going to upset me before my day gets started. I only have five heads to do today and then I am going home and relax."

~

Mike was in the weight room trying to work off the boiling anger he felt flowing through his body.

"I hope that bitch got my letter by now. I wonder if Dink saw her at Pinkeye's party. If he tells me that she was with another niggur, it's ON! She better dismiss that niggur before I get out of here."

Mike counted the money he had in the canteen.

"I have enough to give Duce so that he can get me a package and twirl that shit. Dasha will buy the things I need. She still hasn't been to see me and it's been over a month. If I find out she's fucking around on me, I'll be back here in prison for killing her. If I can't have Dasha, nobody else will."

Just thinking about Dasha made Mike's eyes look wild.

An inmate looked at Mike and said, "Damn man, you look crazy as hell. What kind of shit you on?"

When Mike was a young boy, he was diagnosed as emotionally disturbed. His mother never got medical help for him. She just knocked the hell out of him when he acted up. When he was thirteen, Mike hit his mother in the head with a chair. After that incident, he went from group home to group home—

foster home to detention center—and then to jail. All of his life, he was a troubled child. His parents never stood by him, so he chose the streets as his family. When Mike met Dasha—that was the best thing that had ever happened to him. She took care of him and kept a roof over his head.

"I'll be glad when it's Friday, so I can talk to Dink. He keeps telling me how Dasha's body looks. I hope he is not trying to holler at her, cause if that's the case his ass will be knocked off too."

After he finished working out, Mike felt a little better, but he still had on his mind, the thought of Dasha being with another man. Reality was also setting in—he would soon be getting out of prison.

When a group of inmates walked in, he left the gym.

"Motherfuckers will start something with you when they know it's your time to bag up. I'm gonna keep to myself. I don't won't no trouble to cause me to stay locked up."

~

Duce counted his profit from his crap game. He liked the idea of Pinkeye having card parties twice a month. That would give him a chance to make money.

"I know that Pinkeye is going to have her hand out. Since I don't have anywhere to go, I have no choice but to give her some money.

Damn! That court case is next week. I need to get a court appointed lawyer. I've got to make this money last.

Dink told me that Mike wants me to get in contact with him. I haven't talked to Mike in three years. Knowing him, he's going to make money when he gets out and he's going to want me to twirl a little somethin'. Now that's what's up! Maybe Mike and I can get another place and set up shop and run things like we use to. I need to get Pinkeye to get his address from Dasha.

Speaking of Dasha, she sure has gotten thick. Mike got something good to come home to. Plus, she's making big money. I hope he don't fuck that up."

Duce thoughts broke when he heard Pinkeye calling him. He limped to the kitchen door.

"Damn Pinkeye, you don't have to shout."

"I sorry Boo. I just wanted to know if you are hungry."

"I can eat a little."

"Pinkeye, here's a little somethin' for you and the girls. I am also gonna give my children some money to buy school clothes."

Duce knew that if he did not give Pinkeye a cut, she would damn sure ask.

~

Jackson finished his business meeting, picked up Jaye, and took her out to dinner. He was happy with the business deal he made and was ready to celebrate.

Jaye was feeling Jackson more than ever and planned to show him how much, when they got back to their hotel room. She was impressed with where they were staying—the Hilton Hotel. Before going out to dinner with Jackson, she got a manicure and a pedicure at the hotel's spa.

Jaye's cell phone rang. "Hello."

"Hi Miss Thang," said Jaye's girl friend, Nichole.

"What's up girl," said Jaye.

"Are you in N.Y.C.?"

"Girl you know I am and I did not come all this way to not shop. I need to buy my mother something for her birthday," said Jaye.

"When and where do you want to meet tomorrow?" Nichole asked.

"Let me check with my man and call you back."

"Okay," said Nichole.

Jackson told Jaye to take the limo and have a good time shopping with Nichole. He planned to play golf and lunch with friends while she was shopping.

"Are you sure?" Jaye asked.

"I am sure. I'll make sure that we have the same limo tomorrow."

"Jackson, I will not spend much."

"That's on you Jaye."

"Jackson, I need to pay for my school books. So can I use the credit card for school?"

"You can use the credit card for whatever you want."

After dinner, Jaye and Jackson went back to the hotel. She ordered fresh fruit and Jackson opened a bottle of Ramey Martin. Jaye lit candles in the bedroom and bathroom. She got in the shower and moments later Jackson joined her.

She closed her eyes and felt Jackson's body close to hers. He started kissing and rubbing her ass. She could feel her clitoris pounding. Jackson knelt down and made his way to Jaye's tunnel. The hot water continued to hit Jaye in the face. She let out a sound that turned Jackson on.

She lay back on a tub pillow, while Jackson entered inside her wet clit. The bathroom was filled with steam. The only thing Jaye could see was Jackson handling his business. She screamed and shook out of control. He told her how much he loved her. She kissed him all over his body; she said that she loved him too.

Jackson closed his eyes and felt the emotions that Jaye was giving him. He called her name—over and over again. That really turned Jaye on. Jackson exploded with a feeling that he had never had.

After making love, they ate fresh fruit, had a couple of drinks, and talked for a while. After their third drink, they were feeling good. Jaye felt her clit getting moist again. She climbed on Jackson. She sucked his weak spot—his ear. Jackson could not take it. He carried her into the bedroom for round two. They made love three more times.

Jackson pulled Jaye close to him. He wanted that moment to last forever. Jaye could not believe that she had fallen in love with Jackson.

I know my mother will be happy. With that thought, she fell asleep in her man's arms.

~

Pinkeye used Dasha's car to go shopping. She decided to spend six hundred dollars for her daughters' school clothes—four outfits and high price tennis shoes for each girl.

At the mall, Pinkeye gave her girls twenty dollars for lunch. While they ate, she went into Macy's. She saw a pair of shoes that she wanted. "Damn. If my girls think that I am going to spend every dime on them, they got another thing coming. I will sport these shoes for Christmas."

Pinkeye looked at her watch. It was getting late. She had to go to the grocery store to buy something for dinner, before she took the car back to Dasha. She also wanted to get her nails done at Dasha's shop. Pinkeye hurried to the food court to get her girls. They left the mall.

When Pinkeye made a left turn on Virginia Beach Boulevard, she saw Chicken waiting for the bus. She slowed down and asked him if he wanted a ride? Chicken waved his hand for her to keep going.

"Fuck you," Pinkeye said. "Duce would get mad if he saw me with you any way." Pinkeye sped off. She thought about the court date that was coming up this week. "That's why Chicken's ass brushed me off. I am still going to beat his sister when I see her."

~

Duce made enough money to buy what he considered to be necessities and other important things.

I really need a cell phone to help me move my packages. I got to play it cool so that Pinkeye doesn't find out what I am doing.

Even though Duce was in the streets, he really missed his children. He called his wife and when she answered he said, "I did not call to talk to your ass. Where are my kids?"

"Naw, you ain't talking to nobody," she said.

"Shut the hell up. That's why Pinkeye beat your ass."

"You always taking up for her. You put her before your kids."

"Bitch, nobody comes before my kids, not even your black ass."

Duce heard Pinkeye coming in the door. "Look, don't fuck with me. I am going to buy my kids' school clothes and you better keep them clean."

He hung up the phone when he saw Pinkeye coming down the hall and acted like he was just waking up.

"Hi Boo!" Don't you have something for me?" Pinkeye asked.

"Damn Pinkeye. I gave you money to go shopping."

"Naw, I am talking about a kiss. You don't have a romantic bone in your body. Did I hear you talking on the phone?"

"No. I was just yawning and stretching my body when you came in. When are you planning your next party?"

"Next month. Why?"

"You know I'm trying to help you make money by having a little crap game jumping off in the back room."

"Duce, my girls will be here."

"Can't they stay with Jaye?"

"Every time I have a party, my girls will not go to Jaye's house."

"Damn Pinkeye, you messing up my flow."

"Look Duce, if I have gambling going on in my house every month, it will bring drama. So, NO!"

"Okay. You don't have to shout."

Pinkeye went into the living room and watched TV with her girls.

"Fuck her," said Duce, "I'll make my money while she is at work. I will sell rock during the day and weed at night from her back room window. Damn, that's the way I use to kick it back in the day with Mike and Maleake. By the time Christmas gets here, I will be straight. But I'll still hang in here with Pinkeye, until Mike gets out of prison. I know when Mike gets out—it will be more money, more money, and more money!

Pinkeye thinks that I'm going to get a job. I just told her that so she wouldn't get suspicious about how I was making money. I'll break a little something with her. She's the only lady that gets my money. She puts up with a lot of shit from me—but she is still going to ask for her money."

Duce got up and went into the living room.

"Hi girls."

"Hi Mr. Duce," said Pinkeye girls.

They got up and went to their bedroom. Pinkeye's girls really don't like Duce living with them. A man never lived with them before. Pinkeye noticed the look on her girls' faces, but she did not say anything.

~

Jaye woke up in Jackson's arms. She could not believe what happened last night. She turned over and watched Jackson sleep. She was sure that her feelings had changed for him and she loved it.

Jaye looked at the clock on the wall. She wanted to shower and order breakfast before Jackson woke up. She got out of bed and tiptoed into the bathroom. As the water ran all over her body, it reminded her about the love they made last night. Just thinking about it made Jaye hungry for Jackson.

A sound startled her. She turned around and it was Jackson. He pulled the shower curtain back and joined her.

As Jackson bathed Jaye with a soft sponge, she begged him to make love to her. Jackson pulled Jaye up on him, positioned her body, and slowly went inside of her. Jaye felt light as a feather. She laid back and let him take control. Ecstasy!

After making love, they got out of the shower and dried each other off. Jaye was looking forward to her day.

"What do you want for breakfast?" Jaye asked.

"Surprise me."

Jaye ordered link sausages, pancakes, coffee, fresh fruit, and fresh flowers for a centerpiece. After calling room service, she called Nichole to let her know what time she would pick her up.

After they ate, Jaye and Jackson laid across the bed.

"What do you want for Christmas?" Jackson asked.

"You sound like Monay. She is making plans now for Christmas."

"The reason I asked is because I'm going overseas next month to shop for designer shoes and I wanted to know what you wanted me to bring you back?"

"Where are you going?"

"Paris."

"Yes, I would like it if you could bring me back a designer bag."

Jaye could not believe how things were happening so fast. She got dressed and Jackson called for the limo to pick her up.

Things You Say And Do

Dasha was tired when she got home from the shop. She noticed that she had several messages on her answering machine. While she fixed something to eat, she listened to her messages.

The mortgage company called in reference to her loan. "I hope it is good news; I will give them a call on Monday." She also had a call from Pinkeye who wanted to know if she had heard from Jaye.

Dasha ran her bath water and filled the tub with bubbles. She planned a relaxing evening—giving herself a facial and a pedicure. As soon as she sat in the warm bath water, she felt her baby move.

Dasha reminisced about her mother and the joy that her mother would have felt being a grandmother. For a moment, she felt alone. She had no living blood relatives. But she called Jaye, Monay, and Pinkeye—her family.

After she pampered herself, Dasha lay on her bed and looked through her business folder. She would soon be a mother and it was important to Dasha to have everything in place—business and personal. She took Mike's letter out of her purse and read it.

Dear Dasha,
I hope this letter finds you doing well. You have not been to see me nor sent me money. You know I don't have too many months left in here. I have nowhere to go when I get out and the parole board said that I cannot live in a drug environment. I need you to come and see me. I know I've been demanding but that is going to change. I love you so much. Please answer the phone when I call you this Friday. Take care of yourself.

Always yours,
Mike
P.S. My money is getting low.

Dasha lay back on her pillow and thought about the letter. She wondered how his money was getting low when she had sent him one hundred dollars a week for so many years. But that was no longer her concern since she was not going to visit him nor send him any money.

She set Mike's letter on her bedside table and finished working on her papers. Her telephone rang.

"Hello."

"Why didn't you call me back?" Pinkeye asked.

"Girl, when I got home I took a hot bath and pampered myself."

"Are you okay?"

"I'm fine Pinkeye. Did you make good off your party? Were you able to buy your girls' school clothes?"

"I bought them four outfits."

"Do you need me to help you with anything?"

"Naw, I got it," said Pinkeye. "By the way, I'm planning to quit my part-time job."

"Why?"

"Duce will be living with me."

"Pinkeye, do you think that's a good idea?"

"Dasha, you sound like Jaye."

"I thought you needed money."

"Well, I plan to have two parties a month to make up for quitting my part-time job. Dasha I will give you a call tomorrow. And by the way, don't forget to come for Sunday dinner. Monay is beeping in. I'll talk to you later."

Dasha put her papers away and turned off the lights. While thinking about Pinkeye's good cooking, she fell asleep.

Monay could not wait to tell Pinkeye about the nice things that Maleake did for her. Pinkeye answered.

"Hello."

"Pinkeye you took a long time to answer your phone."

"I was talking to Dasha."

"Did she say why she left the party early?"

"Naw, we did not get into that."

"Well let me tell you about my morning. Maleake cooked breakfast and served it to me in bed."

"You go girl."

"Is he planning on moving in with you?"

"I asked him. He's supposed to let me know by the end of the week."

"I noticed Maleake's been talking a lot to Mike. You know Mike will be getting out in soon. I wonder if Dasha told Mike that she is pregnant," said Pinkeye.

"I don't know. She has not talked about her pregnancy. We need to start making plans for her baby shower. I'm sure Jaye will have it at her house."

"Have you heard from Jaye?" Pinkeye asked.

"Naw, I can't believe she has not called."

"That's not like Jaye," said Pinkeye. "She always calls at least one of us when she is out of town. Maybe she's shopping like crazy with Jackson's money. I wonder what's going on."

Jaye and Jackson awakened after having a romantic night. They ordered room service, got dressed, and packed. While Jaye was in the shower, Jackson opened his brief case and peeped at the fifteen thousand dollar engagement ring that he had purchased at the New York City diamond district. He planned, within the next few months, to ask Jaye to marry him.

After breakfast, Jackson called for the limo to take them to the airport. In the limo, they could not keep their hands off of each other. They were like two teenagers who found love for the first time.

Jaye's phone rang—it was her mother.

"Hi Mom."

"How are you doing baby girl?"

"Mom, I have so much to tell you when I get home."

"What time will you be home?"

"We will be there around noon."

~

Monay wondered why Maleake did not come back last night. She got out of bed and opened her blinds to let the sun in. She decided not to call him or wait for him; she was going to get dressed and go to Pinkeye's for dinner.

She opened her closet to get an outfit to wear. As she was looking through her racks of designer clothes, she noticed that her safe was opened; she also noticed the money that she had saved toward a down payment on a house was missing.

I can't remember opening my safe last night or in the past week. Oh no! Maleake took my money. He is the only person who has been in my house, and he knows about my safe. He'd better have a good reason for taking two thousand dollars. But how did he get the combination?

Monay picked up the phone to call Maleake. No answer. She dialed his number seven times—still no answer. Moments later, Maleake knocked on Monay's door.

When Monay opened the door, Maleake started explaining.

"Before you say anything Monay, I took the money to pay my sister off. When I told her that I was moving in with you, she got mad and demanded the money that I owed her. I will give it back to you."

"Okay, so you are moving in with me?" Monay asked.

"Yes, next week. I've got to finish packing my things."

"Do you need me to help you pack?"

"Naw, I got it. I need you to clear a closet for me. You have your closets on locked down."

Monay hugged Maleake and did not say another word about the money.

~

Mike could not sleep.

"Dasha starts playing games with me and it's almost time for me to get out. I hope Dink got some news about her. I know she was at Pinkeye's party. I don't want Dasha to know when I get out. I am going to surprise her. And when I do, she better have a good excuse for why she stopped sending me money and coming to see me. I refuse to sit back and watch her with another man—and have the fellows on the street talking about that shit. And, if I find out that Jaye had something to do with Dasha not coming to see me, I've got plans for Jaye too."

The more Mike thought about Dasha, the angrier he got.

He sat on his bed and imagined his hands around Dasha's neck. Mike became so upset that he bit his bottom lip. He could taste the blood.

Revenge! Revenge! Revenge! Mike kept saying it over and over again.

Mike has not taken his psychotropic medication in two weeks. He says that the medication slows his thinking process.

~

Pinkeye got up early to start cooking dinner. "I wonder if Jaye is back."

She dialed Jaye's cell phone number.

"Hello."

"What's up Jaye? Are you back home?"

"Jackson and I will board the plane in about ten minutes. Why?"

"Monay and Dasha are coming over for dinner. I thought if you got back in time, you could come too."

"Count me out Pinkeye. You know Ma's birthday is today."

"Oh, that's right. I need to buy her a gift. Did you remind Monay and Dasha?"

"Yes, they both know."

"Are you planning anything for your mother's birthday?"

"Well, I bought her a bag and an outfit from the Chanel Store in New York—and Jackson and I are taking her out to dinner."

"That's nice," said Pinkeye.

"Did you make a good profit from your party?" Jaye asked.

"I did pretty good."

"Tell your girls that I will take them shopping next weekend. Pinkeye, I got to go. Our plane is boarding. I'll talk to you when I get home."

"Have a safe trip."

Pinkeye was puzzled.

"Damn, Jaye was talking nice. She sounded like she and Jackson were married. I got to hand it to Jaye—she sure knows how to get that money."

Duce shouted, "Pinkeye, come in here!"

I'm about tired of Duce's black ass calling me like we live in a big ass house.

"What do you want?" Pinkeye asked.

"Duce, you need to get up and stop calling me every five minutes."

"Damn Pinkeye. There you go talkin' grease shit."

"I was calling you to see if you was cooking breakfast."

"Duce you need to eat a bowl of cereal because I am trying to cook dinner. I invited the girls over for dinner."

"Damn Pinkeye. I don't feel like seeing them."

"So close your damn eyes because they are coming."

"Fuck that shit, I will stay in the back room."

"Well, you do that."

I better be cool with Pinkeye. I need to stay here until I make money. Then I am getting the fuck up out of here.

She opened the oven to put the rolls in and the phone rang.

"Let me speak to Duce." It was Maleake calling.

"You could at least say good morning, you ill-mannered fucker," said Pinkeye.

"My bag. Good morning Pinkeye, can I speak to Duce?"

"Now that's more like it. You know you don't call my house without speaking to me."

"Oh Pinkeye. I heard Harold died. When is his funeral?"

"I don't know. I'm waiting to read about it in the paper. I'm not going around his house fucking with his people. You know they don't like me."

Pinkeye told Duce that Maleake was on the phone. Duce took the phone from her and went in the back room to talk.

"Those two are up to something. I can feel it," said Pinkeye.

"What's up man," said Duce.

"Man I need to get Mike's address."

"I think Dink has it. I was just thinking about Mike and what type of shit he's planning on doing when he gets out," said Duce. "When you drop him a line, tell him to call me."

Duce heard a beep in the phone line.

"Hold on man, this that damn Dasha calling."

"Hurry and get her off the phone," Maleake said. "I need to holler at you about her."

"Hello," said Duce.

"How are you doing Duce?" Dasha asked.

"I am fine. Look here, I got another call. I'll tell Pinkeye you called when I get off the phone." Duce connected back to Maleake. "I'm back. Now, what was that you were saying?"

"Man, Dasha is getting healthy. I think that another niggur is hitting that. Mike might have some problems when he gets out."

"For real-real," said Maleake. "Man have you seen her shop? It looks good on the outside. I heard the inside looks good too."

"Now that's what's up," said Duce. "So man, what's up with us—are we going to do this or what?"

"Man, that's why I need Mike's address. I'll call Dink."

~

Monay started cleaning out her closet to make room for Maleake's clothes.

"I don't want to jump into marriage right away, but Maleake knows that I don't want us to just live together, eventually, I want us to get married."

She thought about how good it would feel to have a child. She also thought about what it would take to buy a new house and take care of a child.

"I know Maleake will not make the kind of money that I make, but as long as he tries to help, I'm okay. I will have my masters degree in nursing next summer. That will boost my salary. I know Maleake will not pass over me for another woman."

Monay and Maleake started dating in high school. Maleake worked a 9–5 job, but he quit and said that he would never work for a white man again. Since then, he has been hustling. He has been with a lot of women, but he always comes back to Monay. At a party, Maleake introduced a woman to Monay. He told Monay that she was his sister, who he lives with. Monay thought that she remembered his sister from high school. Jaye wondered why Monay was just meeting his sister and why Maleake never took Monay to his sister's house.

~

The plane from New York landed on time. Jaye was still on cloud nine. "I hope this feeling never goes away," Jaye thought as she and Jackson held hands walking to baggage claim. After they got their luggage, a sky cap packed their cars and Jackson gave him a generous tip.

Jaye and Jackson kissed—Neither wanted to let go.

"I'll see you this evening at your mother's house."

Giggling like a teenager, Jaye said, "See you at 7:30."

Jaye got in her car, buckled her seat belt, and took out her cell phone to call her mother. Before she could finish dialing, her mom beeped in.

"Hello."

"Hey baby girl. I could not wait for you to call me. What's the good news that you need to tell me?"

"Mom, something happened. Don't ask me what—but I have fallen in love with Jackson."

"What! Are you sure?"

"Yes Mom. Jackson and I are planning to build a relationship together."

"That's nice Jaye. What about all your so-called players? I knew that one day, you would come to your senses."

"Mom, things are working out for me."

"Always keep your hand in the Lord's hands and start going back to church—faithfully. And then, watch how the Lord will bless you, when you put him first."

"Yes Mom," said Jaye.

"I am so proud of you. Maybe Jackson will ask you to marry him."

"Mom, slow down. You're moving a little too fast."

"Maybe you are moving a little too slow. I want grandkids."

"Mom, I just parked in front of my house. I will see you later."

Jaye took her luggage out of her car and went into the house. As she unpacked, she took out her mother's gifts that she bought in New York. *These are wrapped so pretty. Mom is going to be surprised when she opens her birthday presents.*

Jaye checked her answering machine and noticed that there was a call from her doctor. The message was a reminder for her next appointment. *Oh, I had forgotten. I better enter it in my calendar on my cell phone.*

Before she could set a reminder notice about her doctor's appointment, the phone rang.

"Hello."

"What's up Jaye?"

"Who is this?"

"Oh you forgot me?"

"Look don't call my number anymore. I am engaged."
She hung up.
"That's what I will tell these broke ass players from now on."
Jaye changed clothes and put on a pair of jeans and a tank top. Relaxed, she put on a Gerald Albright CD, got a glass of wine, and finished listening to her messages.

~

Dasha got dressed to go to Pinkeye's house for dinner. She wore a full top that hid her stomach. Dasha knew that she still 'had it'! Her customers continued to tell her that she looked good. Some knew that she was pregnant. But Dasha didn't care about that anymore. She was confident that she could take care of herself and her child—even if the father was not in the picture.

Dasha wondered if Jaye was back from New York. She called and Jaye answered on the first ring.

"Hey girl."

"Gee you answered the phone fast. What's going on? Is everything okay?" Dasha asked.

"Yes! Girl, Jackson and I plan to start a true relationship."

"You get out of here. That's good, Jaye. Jackson is a good man."

"I know that now," Jaye said.

"I am so happy for you."

"Dasha, are you going to Pinkeye's for dinner?"

"I am getting ready to go now."

"By the way Jaye, the mortgage company called me. I have to go by there this week. I hope it's good news."

"You don't have to worry. You got the condo."

"I will call you tomorrow. Tell your mother happy birthday for me. I will give you her gift when I see you."

Dasha grabbed her bag and left out the door. She called Pinkeye.

"I have to stop by the store. Do you need anything?"

"Naw," said Pinkeye. "You just hurry and get here."

Dasha drove into the store's parking lot. When she got out of the car, she saw Dink standing in front of the store.

"Hello, Dasha. When's the last time you heard from my boy, Mike?"

"About a month. Why?"

"I was just asking. I see you doing work to your shop. It looks good."

"Thank you."

Dink held the door open for her. As she walked into the store, Dasha could feel Dink's eyes following her.

"Trying to hide my stomach is getting on my nerves. So what if he noticed that I am pregnant."

"Damn! She is looking good," said Dink. "I know Mike is going to want that."

Pinkeye set the table with her good dinnerware. She always liked for her girls to feel special. They always did nice things for each other—even when one might be mad at the other—which didn't last long.

Duce walked into the kitchen.

"Damn. You setting out dinnerware and shit. Who you suppose to be?"

"Duce carry your ass. You don't know nothing about class."

Pinkeye took the food out of the oven and made the final touches to her dinner.

Five minutes later, Dasha knocked on the door. When Duce opened the door the wind blew Dasha's top up. Duce looked at Dasha for a moment before inviting her in. Dasha knew that Duce saw her stomach. She felt really uncomfortable and she was worried about Duce running his mouth in the streets.

"What's wrong with you Dasha?" Pinkeye asked. "Did Duce say something to you?"

"No. When Duce opened the door, the wind blew my top up."

"Did he see your stomach?"

"I don't know."

"Don't worry, if he asks me anything about you being pregnant, I will tell him that you are not."

"Thanks Pinkeye. But I'm getting to the point where it doesn't matter anymore. All I want is a healthy baby."

"I know that's right," said Pinkeye.

Stop the Drama

Pinkeye woke up her daughters and told them to get ready for school. She showered first so the girls could have the bathroom to themselves. When she got out of the shower and went into her bedroom to get dressed, she noticed the bedroom window was opened.

"Damn it!" Pinkeye yelled. Duce sat straight up in the bed.

"What the hell are you screaming for?" He asked.

"Why is my window open?"

"Pinkeye, it was hot in here."

Duce closed the window—that was a sign to his customers that shop was closed. He had been selling crack from that window for a week. He didn't give a damn about Pinkeye and her daughters. Duce was not going to let anyone mess up his game.

Ten minutes after Pinkeye's daughters left for school, the police knocked on her door. When Pinkeye opened the door, an officer told her that they had a warrant for Patricia Miller.

"Are you Patricia Miller?"

"Yes," said Pinkeye. "What is this warrant for?"

"You are charged with malicious wounding of a Miss Brenda Brown," the officer said. "Ma'am, you need to come with us."

Duce heard the officer talking to Pinkeye and went into the living room to see what was happening.

"Can I make a phone call?" Pinkeye asked.

"You can make your call from the police station."

"Duce, call Jaye and tell her what's going on."

"Okay," said Duce.

Pinkeye's neighbors came out of their apartments and watched the police put her into the squad car. Pinkeye thought how glad she was that her daughters had already gone to school.

I would hate for them to see me in handcuffs and hauled off to jail. The nerve of Pea taking a warrant out on me after she stole my got damn money. She's lucky I did not kill her ass.

As soon as the police drove off with Pinkeye, Duce went into the house, walked straight to the back room, and pulled up the window. He was open for business.

Duce never called Jaye to tell her that Pinkeye was arrested.

~

Monay was up late the night before cleaning out closets to make space for Maleake's things. She overslept—so she hurried and got dressed so she could get to work on time.

The day had arrived—Maleake was moving in with her. To celebrate, she planned to cook a nice, romantic dinner. Before she left the house, Maleake called to let her know that he needed her car to finish moving his things in.

"What time can you come by my job and pick up the car?" Monay asked. "Maybe we can eat lunch together?"

"Naw baby. I won't have time. I want to be all moved in before I pick you up from work."

"Okay," said Monay.

Maleake was smiling when he hung up the phone.

"Life is just starting. I got a dumb ass for a woman, and as long as she stays in her place and don't worry the fuck out of me, I can make my money. When she carries her ass to work, I will cook up my rock—then take it to Duce to twirl."

~

Jaye's alarm clock went off and she woke up smiling. She took the day off so that she could go to her doctor's appointment and spend the rest of the day with her mother.

She got out of bed, took a shower, and ate a small breakfast. She didn't have time to check the few messages on her answering machine.

"I'll check my messages later. Probably nothing important—just messages from my old players that I no longer want to talk to."

While Jaye waited to see the doctor, Jackson called and asked her to meet him for lunch.

"Jackson, why would you ask me that? You know that I will meet you anytime—anywhere."

"Well in that case, I will see you later. Love you," said Jackson.

Jackson was nervous about asking Jaye to marry him. He thought about what he would do if she said "no"—he would still love her and ask her over and over again until she said "yes". Jackson thought about their romantic weekend.

"I hope that I'm not moving too fast. Damn, Jaye is good in bed. I want our relationship to last until death do us part."

Jaye walked out of the doctor's office feeling sore, after having a pap smear. "Damn, that doctor hurt me down there."

She got in her car and called Pinkeye to get the news about her selling party. Duce answered the phone.

"Is Pinkeye there?"

"Naw. The police came and arrested her for cutting Pea on Friday night at her party."

Jaye said nothing to Duce—she just hung up the phone.

~

Dasha met with the loan officer before she went to her shop. She could not wait to tell her girls that her mortgage application loan had been approved. She called Pinkeye's house—no answer. Next she dialed Jaye's cell phone number.

"Hey Jaye," Dasha said before Jaye spoke, "guess what?"

"Listen Dasha..." said Jaye.

"I got my mortgage loan," Dasha interrupted.

"That's good. I told you it would go through. Listen Dasha. I am on my way to the police station. Pinkeye is in jail for cutting Pea."

"What! I will meet you there," Dasha said. "I'll call Monay and let her know."

Dasha called Monay at work and told her that Pinkeye was in jail.

"No shit," said Monay, "I will be there in thirty minutes."

Monay told the head nurse that she needed to go home for a family emergency. She left the hospital in a hurry, bumped against a man in the lobby, and kept walking fast. *Damn his face looked familiar.*

When Monay arrived at the police station, Jaye and Dasha were standing outside waiting for her.

"What is going on?" Monay asked.

"Pinkeye has gotten her ass in deep trouble," said Jaye. "I just talked to a bondsman—her bond is ten thousand dollars. I paid it and he is taking care of the paper work. When she gets her ass out, I have a few things to tell her."

"I'm pretty sure Pinkeye feels bad," said Dasha.

Moments later, Pinkeye walked out looking mad as hell.

"I got a court date for next month. The judge is talking about giving me eighteen months in prison."

"Pinkeye, you are still on paper for beating Little Bit half to death. The judge for that case told you that if he saw you in his courtroom again, he was going to give you some time," said Jaye.

"Fuck that. When I see her ass again, I am going to kill that bitch."

"You know what Pinkeye, your ass is going to jail. I knew something like this was going to happen. I could feel the vibe at your party," said Jaye.

"What motherfucking vibe you felt," said Pinkeye. "You kill me with that bullshit. Always thinking like a damn lawyer."

"Will y'all stop arguing," said Monay. "The both of you are making Dasha and me nervous."

"Jaye, I wish I never told Duce to call your ass."

"Duce did not call me. I called your house to talk to you. That's when he told me that your black ass was in jail."

Pinkeye waved her hand at Jaye and walked away.

"That's okay. That stank ass Duce is going to be your downfall, and your daughters are going to be with me."

Dasha started to cry. She begged Pinkeye to listen to Jaye.

"You shut the fuck up with your sneaky ass—walking around here pregnant and Mike isn't the father."

Pinkeye's words hurt Dasha. She walked away without saying a word, got into her car, and drove off.

"I will ride with you Monay," said Pinkeye.

Jaye stood there looking at Pinkeye as she walked away.

Pinkeye got into Monay's car.

"I don't know who in the hell Jaye thinks she is trying to tell me how to handle my business."

Monay kept quiet. She knew if she said anything, Pinkeye would go off, even though she knew Jaye was right.

Monay pulled up in front of Pinkeye's house. Pinkeye saw people standing around the side of her unit.

"What the fuck is going on?" Pinkeye said.

One of the crack heads spotted Pinkeye and alerted Duce.

Duce hurried and pulled the window down.

Pinkeye and Monay went into the house.

"Duce!" Pinkeye screamed. "Why people on the side of my house?"

"What the hell you talking about Pinkeye? I was sleep."

Pinkeye rolled her eyes at Duce.

"Jaye told me you never called her."

"Before I could call the bitch, she called here looking for you and I told her what happened."

Monay's phone rang. It was Maleake.

"Where are you?"

"I'm over Pinkeye's house."

"What the fuck are you doing over there? I am at the hospital waiting for your ass to come out and your black ass is over Pinkeye's. You better bring your ass back to this hospital in ten motherfucking minutes." Maleake slammed the phone down in Monay's ear.

He was talking so loud that Duce heard every word. Duce smiled when he saw how Monay was shaking after Maleake cursed her out. *I wish I could put fear in Pinkeye's ass like that.*

"Pinkeye, I got to go," said Monay. "Maleake is waiting for me."

Jaye could not believe how Pinkeye talked to her. She called Dasha at the shop.

"Hello."

"Hey Boo. Are you okay?" Jaye asked.

"I'm fine," said Dasha. "Pinkeye is off the hook. Ever since Duce moved in with her—she has changed. Pinkeye knows she is going to get some jail time for cutting Pea."

"Hold on a minute Dasha. Chicken is waving at me to stop. Let me see what he wants."

"Hey Squeetie. I just came from court. Duce did not show up, so the state picked up the case and gave my sister five years in prison."

"Dasha let me call you back later."

"Jaye, did I hear Chicken say that his sister got five years?"

"Yes."

Chicken continued to talk while Jaye was talking to Dasha.

"Damn Chicken. Wait until I hang up. I'll call you later Dasha. Now what were you saying Chicken?"

"I was saying that I bought a gun for Duce's ass."

"What! Chicken put that gun away before you hurt somebody."

"I'm going to shoot Duce if he bothers me again."

"Now Chicken, I have told you before that, when you get in trouble you have nobody to blame but yourself. I got to go."

Jaye drove off thinking about Chicken's dumb ass with a gun. As she made a right turn onto Princess Anne Road, she saw Maleake driving Monay's car—speeding down the road.

"She will do anything for his ass." Jaye looked in her rear view mirror and saw Maleake stop in front of a drug spot—he picked up three guys.

"Monay is going to get messed up if she keeps fucking with Maleake. I started to say something to her about Maleake before I went to New York, but that crazy shit that Monay and Pinkeye be talking about their men—I ain't going to sweat it."

Jaye was lost in thought when Maleake sped by again—music loud as hell.

~

Pinkeye sat alone at her dining room table. She thought about how she hurt Dasha's feelings and about what she said to Jaye. Deep down inside, Pinkeye knew she was going to prison— and she knew that Jaye was the only person that she wanted her children to live with while she was locked up.

Duce walked into the kitchen. He could tell that she had a lot on her mind.

"What's up baby?"

"Duce I go to court next month and the judge is talking about locking me up for eighteen months."

"Don't worry, I got your back," Duce said as he kissed Pinkeye on her forehead.

Hearing Duce say that he was there for her made Pinkeye feel better.

~

Dasha could not stop thinking about what Pinkeye said about Mike not being her baby's father.

Her construction crew was putting the final touches on her shop, so she decided to close early. That gave her time to go take care of some business including signing the papers for her mortgage loan.

When she got out of her car in the bank's parking lot, the first person she saw was Dink—sitting in a car with a female. Dink stared at Dasha when she walked by.

"Damn, she's pregnant. Oh shit! I know Mike is not going to like that—his girl pregnant by some other niggur. I know I got to give him a call Friday."

Dasha acted like she did not see Dink. She didn't care if he saw her stomach.

Before she walked into the loan office, her cell phone rang. It was Pinkeye.

'Hello."

"Dasha, I'm sorry for talking to you like that. Will you forgive me?"

"You know I forgive you Pinkeye."

"I also need to call Jaye and apologize."

"That would be nice," said Dasha.

"I love you Dasha."

"I love you too, Pinkeye."

~

Jaye met Jackson at their favorite restaurant in Norfolk's upscale Ghent neighborhood. Jackson smiled when he saw Jaye walk in and greeted her with a juicy kiss. Jaye loved the way Jackson's body felt next to hers. She could feel herself getting hot.

Jaye sensed that Jackson was a little nervous. She began to wonder if one of her old players had told Jackson something. She didn't know what to think. Just when she was falling in love with Jackson—She wanted everything to be perfect.

"Baby you look kind of nervous," Jaye said.

Jackson ignored her comment and asked her if she wanted a drink.

"Not right now."

When the waiter asked for their order, Jackson ordered a glass of Yak and Jaye asked for a glass of water with lemon.

Jackson stared Jaye in her eyes. Jaye's head started throbbing. She just knew that she was getting ready to lose Jackson.

He pulled out a six-carat diamond ring. "Jaye, will you marry me?"

Jaye looked down at the diamond ring. It was the most beautiful ring she had seen in her life. She almost fainted. Her stomach started cramping—her face broke out in a sweat.

"Are you all right? I will take it back if you would prefer another one."

"Hell no! You are not taking this ring."

"So does that mean yes?"

"Yes! Yes! Yes! I will marry you!"

Jackson picked up Jaye and turned her around. The couple that was sitting at a nearby table started clapping.

Jaye could not stop kissing Jackson and admiring her large sparking gold diamond ring.

"Are you going to call your mother?" Jackson asked. "And I know you are going to call your girls."

Jaye took out her cell phone and started dialing her mom's number. She got a beep in the line—it was Pinkeye.

"Hey Pinkeye. Girl, Jackson just asked me to marry him."

"Get out of here," said Pinkeye. "You go girl!"

"I was calling to say I'm sorry for talking to you like I did."

"No problem Pinkeye, I forgive you."

Pinkeye looked at her phone in shock. She could not believe that Jaye did not argue with her.

"Pinkeye, I was just getting ready to call my mother. I'll talk to you later."

"Okay," said Pinkeye.

"Oh Pinkeye. Don't tell Dasha and Monay. Let me tell them. Bye."

Jaye dialed her mother's number.

"Hello baby girl."

"Oh Mom!"

"What's the matter?"

"Jackson just asked me to marry him!"

"Jaye, I hope you said yes."

"I did!"

When a Fool Wakes Up

Pinkeye woke up feeling nervous about going to court. Out of all the times that she had been to court, she had never felt this way before. Monay couldn't get off work, but Dasha and Jaye promised Pinkeye that they would be there.

When Pinkeye arrived at the courthouse, Jaye and Dasha were talking to her lawyer. They all went into the courtroom, and sure enough, Pinkeye had the same judge who told her that if he saw her in his courtroom again, she would get some time.

Her case was second on the docket. The judge lectured Pinkeye about her previous courtroom appearance—then he said, "I sentence you to twelve months in prison." His gavel dropped. It was over. Pinkeye turned and looked at Jaye and Dasha. The sheriff took her by the arm and escorted her to a holding cell. Pinkeye held her head down as she walked out of the courtroom.

"I think Pinkeye kinda felt like she was going to be locked up," Jaye said. "I'm glad she made arrangements for her daughters."

~

Christmas was three weeks away and Jaye, Monay, and Dasha were shopping for dresses for Jaye's wedding. Jaye thought about Pinkeye when she saw a low-cut strapless dress.

"I know Pinkeye would have tried to get me to let y'all wear this for my wedding."

They laughed. Jaye cried.

"I always dreamed that my girls *(meaning Monay, Dasha, and Pinkeye)* would be with me on my wedding day. Now, it won't happen. Pinkeye won't be there."

They all cried.

"This will be the first Christmas, since middle school, that we will not all be together," said Dasha.

"Let's cheer up," said Monay. "Don't forget we are having drinks at my house tonight."

Jaye had forgot all about going to Monay's house. With her wedding two days after Christmas, she had so much to do— including Christmas shopping for Pinkeye's girls.

Damn, I can't stay long at Monay's house. I've got things to do and I surely don't want to sit and look at Maleake and that sorry ass Duce in the face. Duce's black ass did not even go to court with Pinkeye.

I need to make arrangements to put Pinkeye's things in storage soon. I got a letter from her rent office informing me that her things must be out of her unit in one week.

Somebody's been running at the mouth. How did her rent people know that she was locked up? I bet after I kicked Duce's ass out of Pinkeye's house, he went over to the rent office and told everything.

~

The word spread fast around the prison that Pinkeye was there. Pinkeye was surprised to see a lot of people that she hadn't seen in years. Most of the inmates knew her from Church Street, Park Place, and Roberts Park. They knew not to mess with her.

Pinkeye thought about Little Bit and asked her cellmate did she know anyone locked up from Norfolk. Her cellmate told her that there were a lot of inmates from Norfolk. She told Pinkeye that she should ask around at dinner and recreation time. Pinkeye couldn't wait to see Little Bit.

I'm going to beat Little Bit's ass so bad, she's going to wish she was dead.

Pinkeye lay across her cot thinking about her daughters and how much she already missed them. She dozed off to sleep but was awaken by a loud humming sound.

"Shut the hell up!" Pinkeye shouted. "I am trying to sleep."

The humming stopped. Moments later the guards opened the cell doors. Pinkeye did not know what was going on. Her cellmate told her to get up and get in line for dinner. She explained to Pinkeye that they had to line up for all activities— and if an inmate got in line late, she was sent back to her cell.

Pinkeye caught on quick. She knew that she had to follow orders. She did not want to do anything to extend her time being locked up.

When she got to the chow hall, she scanned the room for Little Bit, but she did not see her. Two inmates, who sat next to Pinkeye, started fighting over another inmate.

"Damn. They act like they are going to kill each other over another bitch."

She shook her head and wasted most of her food.

"This surely ain't my cooking."

After dinner, she returned to her cell. An hour later, the guards opened the cell doors for the inmates to go out for recreation. When Pinkeye walked into the recreation room, she looked around the room, but she still did not see Little Bit.

She joined a card game and started talking shit. The same inmate, who was humming when Pinkeye was trying to sleep, started humming again.

"I am getting tired of you humming in my ear. You are breaking my concentration," Pinkeye said.

The inmate continued to hum. Pinkeye's heart started beating fast. When she stood up her legs felt weak and all of a sudden the inmate started singing *Amazing Grace*. She had the most beautiful voice that Pinkeye had ever heard.

Pinkeye's legs started shaking. She jumped up and down—and threw the cards out of her hand. Pinkeye started *Praising the Lord*!

"Oh thank you Lord! Forgive me for my shortcomings. Make me whole. Forgive me for my sins!" Pinkeye shouted.

The guards ran toward Pinkeye. The inmate who was singing, shouted—"Let her be! Praise Him! Praise Him! Give the Lord All of the Praise!"

The inmates who knew Pinkeye could not believe their eyes. The guards stood still. Pinkeye was sweating all over her body and she was crying out to the Lord to come into her life.

"Show me the way to serve you Lord for the rest of my days. I want to serve you Lord!"

The sweat ran into her eyes and blurred her vision. Pinkeye slumped over and hit her head on the edge of a card table. She fell to the floor—unconscious. The guards rushed her to the infirmary.

~

Dasha had about four weeks left before having her baby.

"I'll be glad when Jaye's wedding is over. My body is too heavy. I hope I can wear my gown. It seems like my stomach has gotten bigger since last week."

Dasha was pleased with the way her condo looked. She was glad that Pinkeye had a chance to help her decorate before she went to prison.

She went with the girls to visit Pinkeye, but she had not visited Mike. It had been five months since she talked to Mike or visited him. Now that she had a new telephone number, Mike could not call her at home and threaten her.

Dasha felt safe.

Her phone rang. The voice on the other end said, "Hi Dasha. This is Mike's cousin. He asked me to give you a call to see how you are doing."

Dasha was surprised to hear from one of Mike's relatives. She was so surprised that she hung up the phone.

"I will not let anyone upset me now. So far, I have gone through this pregnancy with no stress, and I am not going to stress out now—when it is almost time for me to have my baby."

Dasha was glad that the girls, especially Jaye, had not questioned her about her baby's daddy. There was a lot going on. She and Monay were giving Jaye a surprise bridal shower; and Monay planned to give her a baby shower a month after she has her baby.

~

Monay was happy to see Maleake move his things in. She had Chinese food delivered for dinner and made sure that he was very comfortable on their first night living together. After they ate, she ran his bath water and laid a pair of silk pajamas on the bed. Monay was so excited.

"Now, Maleake will be next to me every night."

She thought about the money that she gave him to buy a car.

"I will ask him, later, if he got the car."

She picked up her phone on the first ring.

"Hello."

It was Jaye.

"What's this shit that I hear that Maleake moved in with you?"

"Who told you that?"

"Never mind who told me. Is it true?"

"Jaye, I am a grown woman and I can let whoever I want to live in my house. Just like Pinkeye said—you are always trying to run somebody's life."

"Now where is Pinkeye's ass? Locked up in prison behind a no good motherfucker who she called a man. And now your ass is doing the same thing for that sorry Maleake."

"Jaye, you need to stop worrying about me."

"Monay, I just don't want to see you get hurt."

"I will be okay. I told you Maleake is going to ask me to marry him, so be happy for me."

"Okay, I will talk to you later."

Jaye hung up and shook her head. She knew Maleake was not going to ask Monay to marry him. Maleake was up to something. *Chicken was not lying when he said that Maleake was on the corner bragging about his new home with Monay.*

~

Jaye and her mother went to pick out the table centerpiece for the wedding. Just before they walked into the florist shop, Jaye saw Chicken across the street.

He waved and ran over to Jaye and her mother.

"Hi Squeetie. Hi Ms. Scott."

"Hi Chicken."

"Squeetie, I heard you getting married next week."

"That's right."

"Can I come?"

"Chicken if I invite you, I can't have no mess out of you at my wedding."

"Squeetie, I know you are classy. I will not get drunk."

"Well, I am not worried about that because if you come there drunk or get drunk, you will be put out."

Jaye and her mother said good-bye to Chicken and went into the florist shop. They found centerpieces that were a perfect match with the wedding colors—chiffon green with a hint of champagne.

So far, Jaye had spent twenty grand. Jackson told her to buy whatever she wanted for their wedding, and she did just that.

"Ma, I need to get home. The girls will be coming home from school soon."

"Jaye, it is so nice of you to take in Pinkeye's girls to live with you."

"Ma, I wouldn't have it any other way. Those girls have been in my life since they were born and I know they would not want to live with anyone else but me. One of the girls will be going off to college next year and I am going to enroll the other girl into a private high school."

"Jaye, I know you are going to be a good mother when you have children. I can't wait to be a grandmother."

Jaye did not respond.

~

Pinkeye kept hearing someone call Little Bit's name. She turned over and looked at the woman in the bed beside hers; she did not recognize her, but whoever she was, she looked like she was dying. Pinkeye turned over and fell asleep. She woke up and again she heard someone calling Little Bit's name. Pinkeye thought she was dreaming until she saw a nurse walk into the room and say to the woman, "Little Bit, please take your pills".

Pinkeye could not believe it. *Little Bit is only thirty-one years old, but she looks like she is seventy. I know prison time can be hard on some folks, but not like Little Bit is looking. What happened to her?* Pinkeye called the nurse.

"Miss. The patient in the next bed—what is wrong with her?"

"She is a very sick lady," said the nurse.

"She was my next door neighbor. She has only been locked up for a short while."

"Yes. But since she's been in here she has refused to take her medication."

"What is her sickness?"

"She is dying from AIDS!"

The nurse went to see about another patient. Pinkeye's eyes filled with tears. Her heart went out to Little Bit.

Pinkeye slowly got out of bed and stood beside Little Bit's bed. She picked up a Bible from a bedside table and started reading the 23rd Psalm.

Little Bit opened her eyes. She gasped for breath when saw Pinkeye. You would have thought Little Bit saw a ghost. She started to speak, but Pinkeye interrupted.

"Don't be afraid," said Pinkeye. "I am not going to hurt you. The Lord has Saved Me. I am not the same person you knew before. I just want to minister to you."

The nurse noticed Pinkeye reading the Bible to Little Bit. She nodded and walked away.

Little Bit reached out and grabbed Pinkeye's hand.

"What are you doing here in prison?"

Pinkeye told Little Bit what she did to Pea for stealing her money.

Little Bit looked at Pinkeye—straight into her eyes—and said, "Duce took your money, not Pea. He came to the crack house and said that you gave him some money. He bought a package and everybody got high."

Pinkeye broke down and cried—"Lord forgive me for hurting Pea the way I did."

The nurse heard Pinkeye sobbing. She walked over to Little Bit's bed and helped Pinkeye back in bed. Pinkeye asked the nurse if she could come in everyday to feed Little Bit and read the Bible to her.

"I need to check with my supervisor. I'll get back to you on that."

Pinkeye lay in bed looking at the ceiling and calling on the name of Jesus.

"How could Duce do this to me? Lord, take the lusting love that I have for another woman's husband away from me. Cleanse me Lord!"

~

The big day finally arrived for Jaye and Jackson. Before the wedding began—Jaye's mother, Monay, Dasha, and Pinkeye's daughters, all joined in prayer—asking the Lord to bless this marriage. They also said a prayer for Pinkeye. Jaye was pleased to see Pinkeye's daughters looking so pretty in their junior bride maids' gowns, and the girls appeared to be happy.

As soon as Jaye heard the wedding march, her legs started feeling like rubber bands. She inhaled, held it for a few seconds, and then exhaled. Then, with her mother at her side, Jaye entered the sanctuary and gracefully walked down the aisle. She was the most beautiful bride. The guests stood. Their mouths were wide open. They could not believe how radiant

Jaye looked. When she got close to Jackson, he extended his arm and took her hand. Tears streamed down their faces. Everyone could see—in Jackson's and Jaye's eyes—the love they had for each other.

The wedding colors were perfect. The chiffon green and champagne colors set off their skin tones like a tropical glaze of sweet melon and sparkling honeydew. Flowers filled the church from the pews to the front door.

After the ceremony, a reception was held at the Airport Hilton. More than three hundred guests attended the sit-down dinner. There were three limousines for the wedding party. Jackson and Jaye rode in a Rolls Royce that was decorated in their wedding colors.

~

Dasha's back was killing her. She called Monay and told her how she was feeling. "I'll be right there Dasha!" While running out the door, Monay looked at her watch and called Jaye.

Jaye and Jackson should just be getting back from their second honeymoon. I hope their plane landed on time! When Jaye answered, Monay shouted, "Oh thank goodness, you're back! I think Dasha's in labor! Meet me at her house!"

"We're on our way!"

When Monay arrived, Jaye and Jackson were standing on the porch ringing the doorbell. Dasha was in so much pain that she could not get to the door. Luckily, Dasha had given Monay a key to her new house. When Monay opened the door, they saw Dasha on the floor in a fetal position—her water had broken.

Jackson carried Dasha to the car. He sat her on the back seat and laid a blanket over her. He and Jaye rushed her to the hospital. Two hours later, Dasha delivered a seven-pound baby girl. Monay and Jaye were jumping up and down with joy. They now had three girls to spoil—Pinkeye's girls and Dasha's baby.

Jackson looked at Dasha's baby, and wanted—more than ever—to be a father. *I am happy for Dasha, but I wish Jaye and I had become parents tonight. I can't wait until we have our first child.*

~

The rent office gave Jaye an extension—the first week in February to get everything out of Pinkeye's unit. Jaye paid a company to move and store Pinkeye's things. She called Monay and asked her to meet her at Pinkeye's house and help pack up everything.

Jaye arrived at Pinkeye's house before Monay. She saw Chicken sitting on his porch. She waved.

"Hi Squeetie. Can I holla at you? I've got something to tell you about Duce."

"Chicken, I'm really tired. I don't want to hear anything about that sorry ass Duce. I just want to pack up Pinkeye's things and go home."

Several minutes later, Monay drove up. Before Jaye and Monay unlocked the door, Chicken kept nagging and trying to tell them something. But Jaye would not stop and listen.

"Chicken, I'll talk to you later."

When Jaye and Monay walked into the house, they heard someone talking. They walked to the back of the house, and—there was Duce and his crack head friends. The house smelled like days old funk.

"Get your stank ass out of here!" Jaye hollered.

Duce jumped up and said, "I am not going no where bitch. You get the fuck out of here."

Jaye pulled out her cell phone to call the police. Duce grabbed her arm and tried to take her phone. Monay took a lamp and knocked the hell out of Duce. The crack heads ran out of the house.

Chicken heard the noise and ran to Pinkeye's house. When he got there, Monay and Jaye were kicking Duce's ass.

Chicken hollered, "Hold that greasy niggur up."

Chicken pulled out his gun and pushed it into Duce's mouth. He wiggled it around and blood flew everywhere. Monay and Jaye saw the anger in Chicken's eyes. They pleaded with him not to shoot Duce. Chicken snatched the gun out of Duce's mouth. Looking like a wide-eyed dog, Duce ran out of the house.

Jaye then realized that before she and Monay went into the house, Chicken was trying to warn her about Duce.

~

As Dasha held her baby in her arms, she thought about her mother, aunt, and her baby's father. She wanted them beside her. Dasha felt so alone.

Dasha named her baby—Coye Moneta Johnson.

I gave my baby Jaye's middle name. I know Jaye likes that.

Little Coye had some features of her father. Dasha hoped that only she noticed that, and that no one else would notice it for many, many years.

Dasha took a note pad and pen, and started writing Pinkeye a letter.

Dear Pinkeye Girl,
I have a baby girl. Her name is Coye Moneta Johnson. I want you to know...

She stopped writing when Monay walked in.

"Oh Dasha, she is a pretty baby. Please, let me hold her. She looks like somebody I know."

Dasha heart started beating fast.

"You know a baby's features don't look like other people in the family until the baby is older," Dasha said.

Monay really wanted to ask Dasha who was the baby's father, but she decided not to say anything.

"Now that you have a girl, we can have this baby shower and pick out cute little girl's clothes."

Dasha tried not to show the sadness that she felt deep in her heart. She hoped to continue to hide her true feelings. She did not want Monay, or anyone else, to ask questions about her baby's father.

Dasha's thoughts drifted—*I know Jaye and Monay are going to ask me sooner or later. But then again, they might not ask me since they know I don't talk much about my business and that I don't get in their business. I wish Pinkeye were here. I know she would be by my side.*

How a Plan Comes Together

Pinkeye enrolled in a GED program at the prison. She could not believe how fast the time was going by. She dedicated her time to Little Bit and going to school. Sometimes she helped other inmates by reading the Bible to them and having a Bible study session.

All day and night, Pinkeye talked to the Lord—Praising His Name and thanking Him for coming into her life when she needed him the most.

"Mail call," a prison guard shouted. "Pinkeye, come and get your mail." It was a letter from Dasha. Pinkeye had mixed emotions when she read about how well her daughters were doing—living with Jaye. She also wrote about her baby, and other things. Dasha told Pinkeye that she would visit her soon.

Pinkeye's thoughts wandered. She could not wait until the weekend. Jaye promised to bring her girls to visit. Pinkeye had not told anyone that her life had changed—that she was Saved. She felt good about herself and she was not going to let anyone steal the Joy that the Lord had blessed her with. She could not wait to share the good news with her daughters.

Pinkeye also thought about Duce and how she was so glad that he had not visited her. He was the last person that she wanted to see.

Her mind went back to Dasha's letter and the things that she wrote about.

I will pray with Dasha when she comes to see me.

One of the guards came and got Pinkeye. She told her that Little Bit was asking for her. When Pinkeye went into the room, Little Bit reached out her hand. Pinkeye took her hand and prayed. Tears were running down Little Bit's face. Pinkeye could feel the presence of the Lord in the room. Little Bit looked at Pinkeye and smiled—then she closed her eyes and died.

~

All morning, Chicken played gospel tapes. He was singing and shouting all over his house. The sound of the phone broke his spirit.

"Hello," said Chicken.

The person on the other end identified herself as the prison chaplain and told Chicken that his sister died at 11:30 that morning. Chicken did not say a word.

"Sir are you still there?"

"Yes Miss. I am still on the phone. What do I need to do to bring my sister's body home?"

The chaplain gave him all of the details. After hanging up the phone, Chicken fell to his knees and cried. When he got himself together, he called Jaye.

As soon as Jaye got the news about Little Bit, she called Monay. She did not give Monay time to say hello. When she heard Monay pick up the phone, Jaye told her about Little Bit.

"Oh, we've got to go see Chicken," said Monay.

"I was thinking the same thing," Jaye said. "I'll meet you at his house in about an hour."

When Jaye and Monay arrived at Chicken's house, he was crying. He told them that Little Bit's insurance policy would not cover all the funeral arrangements and the cost to bring her body home. Monay and Jaye told Chicken not to worry. They would pay all of the expenses that the insurance did not cover.

Jaye's phone rang. It was her mother.

"Jaye, Pinkeye called. She has been trying to reach you to let you know that Little Bit died."

"Mom, Chicken called and told me. Monay and I are at Chicken's house right now. We are helping him with the funeral arrangements."

"That's nice. Well, I'll call you tonight."

"Okay Mom. I will be home."

Jaye tried to get Chicken to stay at his aunt's house but he told her that he would be all right. After Jaye and Monay left, Chicken got drunk as hell.

The next morning, the news of Little Bit's death spread through Roberts Park, Moton Park, Bowling Park, and Church Street.

When Jaye got home she took Pinkeye's girls to dinner. After the waitress seated them, Jaye told the girls that Little Bit died.

The girls looked at each other and started crying. "Little Bit was our neighbor ever since we were born."

"Girls, I have something else to tell you," said Jaye. "Your mother is calling you tonight at 9:00."

The girls cheered and quickly finished their meals. They wanted to go home and wait for their mother's call.

When they got to the house, the phone started ringing while Jaye was unlocking the door.

"Hurry, Auntie Jaye," the girls shouted.

Jaye ran and answered the phone. "Hello."

"Praise the Lord," said Pinkeye.

Jaye could not believe her ears. Was this really Pinkeye speaking in a soft voice and Praising the Lord?

"Jaye, are you still there?" Pinkeye asked.

"Yes. I'm here. Pinkeye your girls can't wait to speak to you. I know you don't have much time so I'll let them talk first."

Pinkeye was glad to hear her girls' voices. She told them that things would be different when she came home and she planned to move them out of the projects.

"Let me speak to your Auntie Jaye."

"Jaye I will be getting out three months early for good behavior; and I will have my GED when I get out."

Pinkeye also told Jaye that she got Saved and that she was with Little Bit when she took her last breath.

"I will tell you about it when you bring the girls to visit me this weekend."

The operator came on the line. "You have two minutes left to talk."

"Tell my girls, Monay, and Dasha that I love them; and, thank you Jaye, for looking after my girls. I love you."

"I love you too," said Jaye.

"We love you Mommy!" Pinkeye's girls shouted.

~

Little Bit's homegoing was big. Jaye, Monay, and Dasha sat in Jaye's car and watched the crowd walk into the church. They saw people they hadn't seen in years.

"Jaye, is that Duce and his wife going in the church?" Dasha asked.

"Damn sure is. Look at Duce wearing that tight cheap ass fresh water suit and his wife looking a mess," said Jaye. "I told Pinkeye that Duce would go back to his wife—and now Pinkeye is locked up behind his crack head stank ass."

"Look at Ms. James," said Dasha. "She is still going to everybody's funeral, crying harder than the family, eating her ass off, and toting plates of food to her car."

"Dasha you are crazy," laughed Jaye.

"Oh there's Maleake," said Monay, "I'm going to walk in church with him."

Monay got out of the car and slammed the door.

"Damn! She almost took my door off running behind that community penis—sorry ass Maleake. I'd rather hump my thumb than to be with him."

"Come on girl, let's go into this clown ass funeral. No disrespect to the decease," said Dasha.

Chicken was clean. He had on a black suit, a gray shirt with a black and gray tie, and a black pair of Stacey Adams shoes. Just before the service started, Chicken walked up to the coffin, leaned over, gave his sister a kiss, and put something in her suit pocket.

Ms. James pretended that she fainted so all eyes could be on her. People fanned and helped her up. Jaye rolled her eyes, and then laughed when Ms. James's wig fell off.

After the funeral, Jaye walked up to Chicken and told him how good he looked and that his sister's homegoing was nice.

"Squeetie, thank you and your girl friends for helping me out."

"You're welcome. By the way Chicken, what did you put in your sister's suit pocket when you bent over and kissed her?"

"I put a dime bag of weed in her pocket so I will have something to smoke when I join her."

Jaye threw her hands up and walked away.

"I'm just trying to keep it real, Squeetie," Chicken shouted.

"That's too damn real," Jaye shouted back.

~

Jackson and Jaye finally moved into their new home in Chesapeake. Jaye made sure there was plenty of room for Pinkeye's girls, and the house included a mother-in-law suite for her mother—just in case she ever had to come live with them. Of course, the master bedroom suite was on the third floor overlooking the lake. The house was not yet completely furnished. Jaye's mother was helping her select furnishings and Jaye had ordered African art pieces to display throughout the house.

Monay and Dasha picked up Jaye to go shopping. Jaye was happy to see Dasha's baby.

"She is really growing," said Jaye as she held the baby in her arms like it was her own. Jaye's eyes got teary when she thought about what the doctor said at her last check-up.

I'm sorry Jaye, but your test results show that you will not be able to have children.

Monay noticed Jaye. "Are you okay, Jaye?"

"I'm fine. I was just thinking."

~

Jackson felt good about moving into their new house and marrying Jaye. *Things cannot get any better.*

He decided to unpack boxes while Jaye was out shopping. When he picked up a box to take into Jaye's office, it fell out of his hands and papers went everywhere. As he picked up the scattered papers, he saw doctor's records. Jackson read the medical records. The report was from Jaye's doctor stating that she would never be able to have children. Jackson did not believe what he had just read, so he read it again—*you will never be able to have children.*

"She lied to me! She lied to me!" Jackson shouted.

"She used me! She never said anything to me about this! She knows that I want children!"

Jackson felt his blood boiling. He was so upset that he left the house and went to a bar.

~

While they were shopping, Monay bought a bookshelf to display pictures of Maleake and her. She decided to rent a U-Haul truck and ask Chicken if he would help deliver the bookshelf to her house. She called Chicken.

"Hello."

"Hi Chicken. This is Monay. I just bought a bookshelf and I need help moving it to my house. Will you drive a U-Haul truck, pick up the bookshelf, and put it in my house?"

"Sure Squeetie."

"Thanks Chicken. I'm on my way to pick you up."

"I'll be on my porch waitin' Squeetie."

After Monay picked up Chicken, she drove to the U-Haul rental office to pick up the truck. Chicken drove the truck to the store to pick up the bookshelf and then he took it to Monay's house.

When he arrived at Monay's house, the girls were sitting in the car waiting for him. They got out of the car to go into the house. Monay put her key in the lock, opened the door, and heard noise coming from her bedroom.

"Maleake's at work," she said. "I thought I heard something."

She went into her bedroom and could not believe what she saw. Maleake was getting it on in her bed with the girl that he said was his sister. They never stopped. They were so busy that they did not even know that someone was watching them.

Chicken and Jaye came in the house calling Monay's name.

Maleake and the girl jumped up and saw Monay standing there. Jaye and Chicken walked into the bedroom.

"What the fuck," said Jaye.

Monay jumped on Maleake. The girl tried to grab her clothes and run but Jaye pushed her back into the bedroom. Jaye was beating her like she stole something.

Jaye turned around and saw Maleake choking Monay. She knew Chicken had his gun.

"Chicken, give me your gun!" Jaye shouted. "Give me your gun!"

Chicken was standing as stiff as a board. He was looking at the naked woman. "Damn she phat as hell," he said.

"Give me the damn gun, Chicken."

He came out of his trance and hit Maleake in the head with his gun. Monay and Jaye started kicking Maleake.

"I'm tide being a fool!" Monay shouted.

She snatched the gun out of Chicken's hand and put the gun to Maleake's head.

Jaye could see the hurt in Monay's eyes and begged her not to shoot him. "He is not worth it!" Jaye shouted.

"Get out of my house," Monay screamed.

Maleake and the girl did not move.

Monay pointed the gun at the girl and said, "Both of you—get out of my house, NOW!"

Monay chased Maleake and the girl out the front door. She did not even let them get their clothes. Butt naked—they ran down the street. Drivers were honking their horns and driving crazy as hell when they saw Maleake and the girl trying to hide behind trees and parked cars.

Monay went into the house and gave the gun to Chicken.

~

When Jaye got home, Jackson was sitting on the floor in the family room—he was drunk as hell.

"Jackson, you've been drinking. You are drunk!"

Jaye started telling him about what happened at Monay's.

Jackson staggered up and said, "I don't want to hear that shit."

"What is wrong with you?" Jaye asked.

Jackson gave Jaye the papers that he found. Jaye covered her mouth—she didn't have to read the papers. She knew what they were.

"Jackson, let me explain," she pleaded.

"Jaye this is your last time making a fool out of me. I'm tide being a fool!"

He went upstairs and threw some clothes in a small suitcase. Then he came downstairs and said, "You will be hearing from my lawyer."

Jackson left.

Jaye fell to her knees—crying her heart out.

~

Mike was nervous. He could not believe the day had come for him to get out of prison. No one but his sister knew that he was getting out. All kinds of thoughts were on his mind.

One thing I know—I am going to take care of Dasha first. I will follow her home to see where she lives and then make my move on her.

As he waited in the discharge room, a guard gave Mike his papers and the name of his probation officer who he needed to report to three days after his discharge. The guard also talked to Mike about wearing the ankle bracelet. Mike hated the idea that he had to wear something to track his every move.

From the discharge room, a guard took Mike to the release room. Across the room, he saw his sister looking out a window. Mike called out her name. She turned around and saw Mike. She could not believe how good he looked. They hugged.

On the way home, Mike's sister told him about what was going on in the streets and that the fellows were asking when he was coming home.

"I hope you did not tell them anything," said Mike.

"I did not tell anyone. So what are your plans, Mike?"

"I have a little money saved so that I can get back my drivers license and buy a car. Have you seen Dasha?"

"No. But someone told me that she had a baby."

"So it's true what Dink told me. So what did she have?"

"I think she had a girl."

She told him that she heard that Dasha bought a nice condo close to McArthur Mall.

"What's McArthur Mall?"

"Oh, that's the new mall across from Tidewater Park. I will take you to see it later today."

She drove Mike by the old hood. He saw a few people, who he knew, standing on the corner. He ducked down so they could not see him.

"Damn," Mike said. "What happened to Bowling Park?"

"They tore it down and Roberts Park is next to go. The old Church Street is also gone."

"Damn," said Mike, "things have really changed."

~

Pinkeye was elated that she passed her GED test. Now she could study to be a preacher. She read the Bible day and night—she wrote scriptures and quotes. Some of the inmates came to Pinkeye for prayer—some cried—some just wanted to talk.

Since she was *Saving Souls*, the guards gave Pinkeye more freedom than the other inmates.

She shared her life story with the younger inmates who did not have a clue as to what life was all about. Pinkeye also had permission to give religious materials to her fellow inmates. She bought the materials with some of the money that Jaye, Monay, and Dasha sent her monthly.

Every Sunday, Pinkeye had church—teaching and preaching the gospel. After service, she always thanked the Lord for Saving her. Pinkeye also asked the Lord to look over Dasha and her baby, and to help Dasha through what she wrote about in her letter. Pinkeye had one more month to serve in prison. She could not wait to get out and be there for Dasha. From the letter, she knew that Dasha needed her.

A guard came to Pinkeye's cell and told her that she had a visitor.

"Who is it?"

"It's a gentleman."

Pinkeye went to the visitation room and saw Duce—all smiles. When Duce hugged her, he noticed that there was something different about her.

Pinkeye pushed Duce away.

"Duce, I am not the same person you knew eight months ago. My life has changed. I Am Saved Now! Before Little Bit died, she told me that you stole my money, and that she and Pea got high with you. She also said that you told them that I gave you the money."

"That dead bitch lied."

"That's enough Duce. I've been a fool for you too long. I never want to see you again. I'm tide being a fool!"

Pinkeye called for the guard to carry her back to her cell. Duce tried to play it off.

"Oh! You will be running back to me when you get out."

But Duce had never seen Pinkeye like this before. He knew that she was not playing.

~

Jaye was so right about Maleake. He never loved me; he only made a fool out of me. I gave him everything. He never gave me nothing but a wet ass. How could I be so blind? Now that I have Maleake out of my life, I will never be another man's fool.

Monay's phone rang constantly for more than an hour but she never answered. Every time she looked at her caller ID, it was Maleake.

"What the hell does he want?" Monay screamed. She finally decided to answer.

"Hello. What do you want Maleake?"

"I want my clothes and I want to talk to you about what happened today."

"Fuck you! You are not coming to get a damn thing. I put your shit in the trash!"

"What! I am going to kick your ass."

"You must have a memory loss. I bought everything you wore on your stanking back."

"You weak bitch. I am coming over to your house right now."

"You can come over here if you want to but I will bust a cap in your ass."

Monay hung up the phone and finished getting Maleake's things out of her house. While pulling his clothes out of her closet, a pocketbook fell open on the floor. Monay bent down to pick up the stuff and saw a business card of a Dr. James Smith, MD. She put the card on her bedside table.

Who is Dr. Smith? When and where did I get this card?

Look At Me Now

Jaye drove to her mother's house, crying all the way. She could not believe that Jackson left her.

"I should have told him the truth. I've been the biggest fool of them all. I had it all—a good man that loved me—and all I did was take his kindness for weakness."

When she pulled in her mother's driveway, Jaye sat in her car for a while. She hoped when she walked into the house—her mother and the girls would not notice her tear stained eyes.

She opened the door and heard the television.

"Hey guys," said Jaye as she walked into the family room.

"Hi Auntie Jaye." The girls' eyes were set on the television.

But her mother looked up and could tell that something was wrong.

Jaye walked out of the room. Her mother followed.

"What's the matter Jaye?"

"Ma, Jackson left me and he said he wants a divorce."

"What happened Jaye?"

"Ma, there is something that I never told you. I can't have children. My doctor told me when I went for a physical six months ago."

She laid her head on her mother's shoulder and cried.

"Jackson found the doctor's papers in a box when he was putting things away. I was going to tell him. Ma, I have been a big fool. You told me that one day things were going to come back and haunt me."

"Stop crying. Jackson is talking out of anger. Things will work out. He loves you too much."

"Ma, I've never seen him act like that. I don't think he will take me back. I should have told him the truth."

~

Maleake picked up Duce to go with him to get his clothes from Monay's house. They started talking and bragging about the guy they robbed last week. They took his dope package and money.

When Maleake turned the corner to cut through Park Place, two cars blocked him in. The sound of gunfire exploded. The gunmen drove away.

Duce got out of the car and ran down the street. Maleake's limp body lay on the steering wheel—he was dead. Duce kept running until he collapsed in the middle of the street.

When Duce woke up in a hospital, he felt strange—different. He got scared and became hysterical.

"I have no feelings in my legs. Help! Somebody help me!"

A doctor walked into Duce's room and tried to calm him. He told Duce that he was paralyzed from the waist down.

"Paralyzed!" Duce said. "Paralyzed! Not me! I got to walk. I got to!"

The doctor told Duce that he had been in the hospital for three weeks.

"Three weeks!" Duce said.

"Is there anyone at home who can take care of you?"

"Yes, my wife. Has anyone called to let her know that I am in the hospital?"

"Yes, our discharge nurse called and your wife informed us that you could not come to her house and that she had filed for a divorce. Is there anyone else that we can call?"

Duce held his head down in shame. "No, there is no one. I have no one that I can stay with."

The doctor told Duce that he would have to wear a colostomy bag for the rest of his life.

Duce was sent to a nursing home.

~

Dasha picked up little Coye from the sitter when she got off work. She could not wait to get home to feed Coye and settle in for the night. When she drove into her garage, she heard something but when she looked around—she saw nothing. Dasha quickly gathered her things, took the baby out of her car seat, and went into the house.

Mike borrowed his sister's car and followed Dasha home. Seeing Dasha with another man's child made him furious. All he could think about was killing Dasha.

Mike was ordered to check in with his probation officer three days after he got out of prison, but he never did. As a result, his probation officer put an arrest warrant out on Mike—but Mike didn't care. His anger for Dasha controlled his mind.

Thirty minutes after Dasha was home, she got a call from Pinkeye who told her that Mike was out of prison. Dasha's heart started racing. She was in shock. She thanked Pinkeye for telling her and told Pinkeye that she would call her in a few days.

As soon as Dasha hung up the phone, she checked on her baby. She thought about the gun that she bought and registered about a year ago. She got it for protection but never thought that she would ever have to consider using it. But after hearing about Mike getting out, she knew that she had to protect her baby and herself. Dasha went to her bedroom and took her gun out of a box in her closet. She made sure it was loaded.

~

Jackson really messed up my head. Jaye could not believe this was happening.

My classes start this week and I can't concentrate. I hope Pinkeye understood when I told her why I did not bring her girls to see her last weekend. I'm glad Pinkeye is getting her life together. She sounds so peaceful on the phone. I was happy to hear that she is coming home this week. I need to make room for her to stay here with me and her girls.

Jackson continued to make the house mortgage payments. He was glad to hear that Pinkeye was coming home. He agreed to let Pinkeye stay with Jaye until she could afford to get an apartment.

The sound of the phone broke Jaye's thoughts.

"Hello."

"Hi Jaye. Can you watch the baby for me today?"

"I would love to Dasha. What time will you bring her over?"

"I will be there in an hour."

"Okay. I will see you then."

Jaye thought about Dasha and how she had balanced her life between being a single mother and owning a business. "Dasha is a good mother. Although she runs a business, she spends a lot of time with her baby."

Jaye heard someone putting the key in the door. It was Jackson coming in. He had divorce papers for her to sign.

"I'm not going to trip. I have tried to talk to him for three weeks and got no rezones from him. I will hurry and sign the papers. I want him gone before Dasha and the baby get here. As close as I am to Dasha and Monay, I'm not ready to tell them that Jackson and I are getting a divorce."

Jackson gave Jaye the papers. She went into the kitchen to get a pen. The doorbell rang. It was Dasha and her baby.

Jackson opened the door and did not waste anytime asking Dasha if he could hold her baby.

As soon as Jaye walked into the room, jealousy tingled through her veins when she saw Jackson holding Dasha's baby. For that moment, he looked happier than she had ever seen him. Jaye tried not to show her emotions about the baby, the divorce, or Jackson, but Dasha noticed Jaye's expression and sensed that something was wrong. Dasha hugged Jaye and hurried out of the house.

Jackson asked Jaye if the papers were signed. She gave him the signed divorce papers. Jackson put the baby in Jaye's arms and left.

~

Monay thought about the phone call she received from an old high school friend telling her that Maleake was killed in Park Place. She was sad, but she could not get over him having another woman in her bed. She decided not to attend Maleake's funeral. She felt lonely.

Monay reached for the phone to call Dasha and saw Dr. James Smith's business card.

"Damn," she said. "Now I remember. He's the one that I met in the parking lot at the mall. It's been months since I saw him. He might not remember me."

She dialed.

"You have reached the voice mail of Dr. James Smith. I'm currently out of town. If this is an emergency please contact Dr. Brown, who is seeing my patients during my absence. Thank you."

"Hi Dr. Smith. This is Monay. I met you at the mall about seven months ago. We were going for the same parking space. Give me a call."

Dasha put the phone down and said, "I probably missed my blessing messing around with that low life Maleake. All those years—I let him make a fool out of me."

~

Mike parked across the street from Dasha's shop—waiting to make his move on her. It looked like all of her customers had gone, so he got out of the car and went to the back of the shop. He broke a window and climbed through it, but what he did not know was that a customer was in the bathroom.

Dasha heard glass shatter. She turned around and saw Mike standing in the hallway. The look on his face told her to run.

"Don't back away now. I've been following you since yesterday and I know you got a baby by another niggur. Dasha, what you take me for—a damn fool?"

"Mike, you been gone for ten years. What did you think I was suppose to do?"

"Bitch, you were coming to see me and sending me money every week and then all of a sudden you stopped."

"Mike I did good by you for nine years. I have a child to take care of now."

"Fuck that shit!" Mike screamed.

"Get away from me!" Dasha hollered.

The customer in the bathroom heard Mike and Dasha fussing and dialed 911 from her cell phone.

Mike grabbed Dasha and started choking her. Dasha did all that she could to get away from him. She kicked him in his private—Mike fell to the floor. She ran toward the front door. Mike pulled out a gun.

Bang! The bullet went in Dasha's back but she kept running.

"If I can't have you, nobody will!" He shouted.

Bang! He shot her again. She fell to the floor. As the blood poured from her body, Mike stood motionless.

Ten minutes later after the customer dialed 911, the police surrounded the building.

Mike panicked and shot through the window. The police ordered Mike to give himself up.

"If ya'll motherfuckers want me, then come and get me!"

The police shot tear gas in the building.

Mike ran out of the building shooting.

The police fired numerous rounds hitting every part of Mike's body. Clutching his gun—Mike died.

The police stormed into shop.

The customer heard the police and cautiously opened the door. She saw the paramedics put Dasha on a stretcher and load her body into the ambulance. Before she could get outside, the sirens started—Dasha was rushed to the hospital.

~

Jaye was wondering why Dasha had not called.
That's not like Dasha not to call and check on her baby.
Jackson could have melted when he saw Dasha's baby. I know he wished the baby was ours.
Jaye started crying. *We could adopt. There are lots of children in the system that are waiting to be adopted. And with me being a social worker—it would be easy.*
Jaye decided to give Jackson a call to talk to him about adoption. Before she could finish dialing his number, she heard a beep in the line. She answered—it was the police telling her that she was needed at the hospital right away. There had been an accident involving Dasha.
"Oh my God!" Jaye screamed. "I will be right there."
She called Monay and told her about Dasha. Monay jumped in her clothes, grabbed her purse, and headed out the house. She looked in her purse to get her cell phone to call Jaye. It was not there so she went back into the house to get it.
She opened her front door and heard her phone ringing.
"Hello."
"Hi Miss Monay. This is Dr. Smith returning your call."
"Dr. Smith, can I call you back. I am on my way to the hospital. I just got a call that my best friend was in an accident."
"What hospital is your friend in?"
"She was taken to Sentere Hospital."
"I will meet you there."
Jaye left the baby with Pinkeye's girls and raced out of the house. When she got to the hospital, Monay was getting out of her car. She honked her horn and told Monay to wait for her. Holding on to each other, they rushed into the emergency room—calling out for Dasha. A doctor walked up to them and asked their names.

"I'm Jaye. This is Monay. The police called me and said that Dasha was in an accident. What happened?"

"She was shot in the back twice and lost a lot of blood. Her pulse is very weak."

"Shot!" Monay yelled. "What happened? Can we see her?"

"I don't think that would be good," said the doctor.

Monay and Jaye demanded to see Dasha, but the doctor insisted that they couldn't. At that moment, Dr. James Smith walked up and spoke to the ER doctor. Dr. Smith told him that it was okay and that he would go in with the ladies. The ER doctor agreed.

When Jaye and Monay walked into the room, Dasha was drifting in and out—but she recognized her girls. She reached out for Jaye.

Jaye took her hand and Dasha spoke with a faint voice. She was trying to tell Jaye something.

"Jaye. Jaye." She kept calling Jaye's name. "Please forgive me."

"I'm right here," said Jaye.

Jaye put her ear close to Dasha's lips—trying to hear what she was saying.

"Jaye, please take care of my baby and forgive me for what I have done. Jackson is my baby's father."

Dasha closed her eyes and died.

Monay screamed to the top of her voice. Dr. Smith grabbed her in his arms and held her tight.

Jaye could not move. She stood there looking at Dasha's peaceful body, then she ran out of the room.

Monay dreaded calling Pinkeye to tell her about Dasha. When she heard Pinkeye say hello, she broke down and cried. It hurt her so much to tell Pinkeye that Dasha was dead.

"What is going on?" Pinkeye asked. The first thing that came to her mind was that something had happened to her girls. Pinkeye's heart started racing.

"Monay, are my girls okay?"

"Yes, your girls are fine but..."

"But what," Pinkeye interrupted, "what is it?"

"Dasha was killed. Mike shot her."

Pinkeye dropped the phone and fell to her knees.

A guard picked up the phone and asked Monay what was going on? Monay told the guard what happened to their best friend.

"Please stay with Pinkeye. We all are like sisters."

"She will be fine," said the guard. After the guard hung up the phone, he helped Pinkeye stand up and walked her back to her cell. Pinkeye started saying the 23rd Psalm.

~

The day arrived for Pinkeye to be released from prison. Jaye took Pinkeye's girls with her when she went to pick up their mother. During the two-hour drive, Jaye never said a word. She kept hearing Dasha's voice. The girls knew that something was wrong with Auntie Jaye, but they did not say anything.

When they got to the prison, Pinkeye was standing outside waiting. The girls got out of the car and ran to hug their mother. Jaye stayed in the car. When Pinkeye got into the car, she could tell that Jaye had a lot on her mind. During the trip home, Pinkeye and her girls talked, but Jaye did not join in the conversation.

When Jaye got home, she went straight to her bedroom and closed the door. Moments later, Monay called to find out what day and time they were going to meet with the funeral director.

"I am not going," said Jaye. "You and Pinkeye can take care of the arrangements."

Monay did not say anything. This was not the time to argue. Three days had passed since Dasha was murdered. They were all grieving in different ways. Monay had not eaten in three days.

I know that I need to get myself together. Maybe Pinkeye can change Jaye's mind. I can't wait to see Pinkeye. I'm going over to Jaye's house, right now.

Fifteen minutes later, Monay arrived at Jaye's house. She and Pinkeye hugged and cried. Jaye didn't come out of her bedroom.

"Pinkeye, I don't know what's going on with Jaye. Ever since we left the hospital, she has not been right. Dasha kept calling Jaye's name and Jaye put her ear close to Dasha's mouth to hear what she was saying. When Dasha closed her eyes, Jaye stood there like she saw a ghost."

Pinkeye put her head down.

Monay wondered why Pinkeye didn't say anything.

They left and went to the funeral home.

"That was the hardest thing that I have ever done," said Monay. "I don't know how I am going to get through this funeral."

"Dasha is in a better place," said Pinkeye. "She is looking down on us."

"Do you think Jaye is going to be okay?"

"Give her time Monay. Jaye is having a hard time dealing with things. She will come around."

~

Dasha lay in a mahogany wood coffin. She was dressed in a beautiful cream color suit. There were so many flowers from her customers. She looked so peaceful—she looked like she was asleep.

Pinkeye, Monay, and Jaye were allowed to be alone with Dasha a half hour before the funeral started. Jaye sat and stared at Dasha. She showed no emotions. Dasha's baby started crying. Jaye walked over to Pinkeye's daughters, took the baby, and kissed her soft cheeks. Then Jaye broke down and cried.

People lined up around the block to attend Dasha's funeral. The church was packed—standing room only. Some of the people there did not even know Dasha—they just came to be nosy.

When the funeral procession started, hands went up and mouths flew open. Folks were shocked. Pinkeye, the noted project bully and man hustler, was leading the procession.

Folks that Pinkeye hung with years ago could not believe it—Pinkeye in a preacher's robe! The old folks in the neighborhood were proud to see—the changed Pinkeye.

Pinkeye Preached and Saved Souls. At the end of the eulogy, she saw Pea standing at the back of the church. Pinkeye walked up to Pea, took her hand, and brought her to the front of the church. Right there, in front of everyone, she asked Pea to forgive her. They hugged and both began to cry.

Pinkeye shouted up and down the aisles. The spirit of the Lord guided her like she was an angel.

Pea fell to her knees and asked the Lord to come into her life.

"Take the drugs away from me. Take the drugs away from me." She kept saying it over and over again.

Pinkeye looked up and saw Jackson walk into the church. Jaye turned around, and saw Jackson. She ran to him and put the baby in his arms.

Jaye went to the altar for prayer. Pinkeye asked Jackson to join Jaye at the altar. When Jackson got to the altar, Pinkeye reached in her pocket and gave him a letter. Pinkeye asked the church to pray with her for Pea, Jaye, Jackson, and the baby.

After the funeral, Monay and Pinkeye went to Jaye's house. Jackson was sitting in his car in the driveway. They waved to him and went into the house.

Jackson took the letter, that Pinkeye gave to him in church, and began reading:

Dear Pinkeye,

By the time you get this letter, I hope you are doing well. I miss you so much. You are the only one that I can talk to about the things that are going on in my life. Lately, there have been a lot of things on my mind.

I never told anyone about my baby's father. It hurts so much to talk about it. One thing that I can truly say is that my baby was made out of love.

Pinkeye, please don't judge me to be a bad person after I tell you this—Jackson is my baby's father.

One evening Jackson came to my shop to talk about Jaye. I was getting ready to go home and he really looked like he needed someone to talk to, so I invited him to my house for a drink. One thing led to another. All the time that we were making love, he kept calling Jaye's name.

Pinkeye, before that night, it had been nine years since I'd been with a man. Jackson's touch was so gentle. I wished that Mike would hold me in his arms that way.

After we finished, Jackson got dressed and he apologized over and over again. We vowed to never speak a word about what happened. Jaye is a lucky lady but she doesn't realize how lucky she really is. For a brief moment that night, I wanted to be Jaye.

Jackson does not know that the baby is his and I don't know when will be the right time to tell him.

Love,
Dasha

When Monay and Pinkeye looked out the window, Jackson was gone.

~

Jaye woke up early the next morning. Pinkeye sat at the kitchen table drinking a cup of coffee. She watched Jaye as she moved around the kitchen.

"Pinkeye we need to talk," Jaye said. "There is so much that you need to know."

The doorbell rang. It was the mailman with a certified letter for Jaye. She signed for the letter. She thought it was a letter from Jackson's lawyer about their divorce; but it was a letter from Dasha's lawyer requesting to meet with Jaye, Monay, and Pinkeye.

The next day they went to the lawyer's office. He read Dasha's will. She left one hundred grand each—to Jaye, Monay, and Pinkeye. Dasha willed her shop and her house to Pinkeye, but left Jaye in charge of everything for two years; she felt that would give Pinkeye time to get her life in order. Dasha also left a trust fund for her daughter, which she couldn't touch until the age of twenty-one.

"Miss Jaye Scott," the lawyer said, "Dasha's wishes were for you to raise her daughter."

Jaye did not respond.

They all left the lawyer's office stunned.

"I did not know Dasha was rolling like that," Monay said.

"Me neither," said Pinkeye.

Jaye didn't say anything. Pinkeye looked at Jaye and shook her head.

Two weeks later, an insurance agent called Jaye and asked her to come to his office. Jaye went over immediately and was told that Dasha made her beneficiary of more than one million dollars. Jaye signed the papers and left. Driving home—she cried. With all the money that she now had, Jaye was not happy. She felt alone and empty.

When Jaye got home, Jackson was there. As she walked up the driveway, he and Pinkeye came out of the house. Jackson, with tears in his eyes, handed Dasha's letter to Jaye. She stood there and read the letter. Jackson told her that he never meant to hurt her.

"Jaye, can you find it in your heart to forgive me?"

"Jackson, we both made mistakes and I was the biggest fool of all."

He grabbed her—kissed her—and said, "I love you so much."

Jaye held him tightly and told Jackson how much she loved him. When she took her arms from around him, she fainted.

Pinkeye ran to Jaye's side and started praying. Jackson carried Jaye into the house. She felt sick when she woke up. She lay in Jackson's arms with their baby in her lap.

The next day Jackson took Jaye to the doctor. The doctor examined her and asked Jaye to take a seat in his office. Jaye was so nervous—she walked back and forth—she could not sit down.

"Whatever it is," Jackson told her, "we will get through it together."

When the doctor walked in, Jaye was about to fall apart.

"Well Mrs. Weatherspoon, you are three months pregnant."

"WHAT!" Jaye said.

Jackson jumped in the air and picked up Jaye.

"This calls for a celebration," he said.

They ran out of the doctor's office and started dialing their cell phones. Jackson called his friends and Jaye called her mother and her girls—Monay and Pinkeye.

Everyone couldn't wait to spread the good news!

Epilogue

On a cool winter day, a calm breeze embraced the girls as they walked through the cemetery. The ground was soaking wet from a thunderstorm the day before. The thick mud slowed their anxious pace to their beloved's graveside.

Finally there—
They held each other by the arm.
One by one they kneeled.
Then, one said a prayer.
And in unison—
They kissed the headstone and said—
"Rest in peace—until we meet again."

Books by O.L. Hall

Tide being a fool

Tide being a fool:
When a Whore Gets Tired

Upcoming Sequel

Tide being a fool:
Mama I Got Your Back

About the Author

O.L. Hall is a native of Norfolk, Virginia. A graduate of Norfolk State University, she has a bachelor's degree in social work and a master's degree in counseling.

When Hall is not working on her book series, she enjoys interior decorating, cooking, and spending time with her family.

She and her husband reside in Chesapeake, Virginia. They have one daughter.

For information about ordering copies of *Tide being a fool* and other books by O.L. Hall, visit www.Tidebeingafool.com.

www.ingramcontent.com/pod-product-compliance
Lightning Source LLC
Chambersburg PA
CBHW051832090426
42736CB00011B/1772